The
Federal Funds
Market

ITS ORIGIN AND DEVELOPMENT

by
PARKER B. WILLIS

Published by
THE FEDERAL RESERVE BANK OF BOSTON
1970

First Edition, 1957
Second Edition, 1964
Third Edition, 1968
Fourth Edition, 1970
Fifth Edition, 1972

PREFACE

Since its first publication in 1957, *The Federal Funds Market — Its Origin and Development* has been reprinted on several occasions to meet the requests of teachers, students, and money market participants thoughout the Nation.

Because the Federal Funds market has shown such remarkable growth and development and because public interest in the topic continues to increase, we are pleased to present this revised, updated, and expanded treatment.

The Federal Funds market evolved in the early 1920's as an informal by-product of the organization of the Federal Reserve System. It began with the trading of reserves by several of the System's New York City member banks as a means of adjusting their reserve positions.

In 1957, average daily purchases were slightly more than $1 billion. Currently — on some days — these purchases are estimated at between $10 and $15 billion. Some 350 banks are now regular participants in the market, while close to 3,500 banks buy or sell Federal Funds at least once a year, more than twice the number in 1960. The market during the last ten years has experienced considerable change in both structure and institutional practice. In addition to serving its original purpose, the Funds market has long been well established as a major outlet for short-term investment of secondary reserves, and it continues to finance, both directly and indirectly, much of the operations of Government security dealers.

Although it is growing, the body of literature concerning this important facet of our Nation's financial structure remains relatively small. This study is designed to increase general knowledge of the Federal Funds market, to clarify its relation to other money market instruments, and to illustrate its contribution to the smooth functioning of the American economy.

We hope this revised edition will lead to a broader understanding of the American money market and will continue to stimulate interest in its successful operation.

FRANK E. MORRIS, *President*
Federal Reserve Bank of Boston

November, 1970

CONTENTS

CHARTS AND TABLES

The Federal Funds Market

ITS ORIGIN AND DEVELOPMENT

INTRODUCTION

The Federal Funds market is a specialized product of American financial organization. Prior to the formation of the Federal Reserve System, the American short-term money market included only commercial paper and call and time loans on security collateral at the New York Stock Exchange. Large correspondent banks in New York City and elsewhere were substantial lenders on security collateral. The smaller banks, on the other hand, traditionally placed the bulk of their short-term liquid funds in the open market for commercial paper or on deposit with the New York banks. Interbank deposits served as an important auxiliary to these markets, and to the extent that interest was paid on the deposits, they served as a direct means of investment by the depositing bank as well as a channel through which the ultimate investment was made. For a number of banks, they served, in part, some of the purposes that sales of Federal Funds later came to serve. Although these sectors continued to dominate money market activity even after 1914 — retaining their traditionally broad character — new instruments were introduced that would eventually supersede them in importance.

The financing of World War I inaugurated a market for short-term U.S. Government securities. As the Reserve System developed, it encouraged and supported the organization of an acceptance market, which by 1918 had completed its basic framework. Now almost 50 years old, the market for Federal Funds emerged as a by-product of the Reserve System organization imposed on the unit banking structure. At the beginning of the 1920's, it became a "new market" within that group of institutions known as the money market.

Federal Funds are immediately available Federal Reserve Funds and are essentially titles to reserve balances of member banks at Federal Reserve banks. Initially, the term, as generally used, referred to the amount of reserve balances that member banks held in excess of legal requirements and were willing to lend to banks having reserve deficiencies. Currently, however, the term more accurately means simply reserve balances borrowed or loaned.

1

Today, some banks will deliberately run "short" on their reserve positions by lending reserve balances to other banks, thus causing or sometimes even increasing a daily deficiency that they expect to cover later in the reserve period. Usually, Funds transactions are for overnight, and the rate of interest is negotiated or determined by the demand and supply of funds in the market. On the other hand, some banks depend on this market as a source of funds for carrying an overinvested position for varying lengths of time.

In substance, Funds transactions are borrowings or loans of reserve balances. In practice, they are described as purchases or sales. The market cannot increase or decrease total member bank reserves but only redistributes them, providing a fuller use of bank reserves and resources.

Roughly similar in concept to the very early Funds market is the arrangement found at the Boston Clearing House between 1880 and 1910. During this period, the custom developed of borrowing and lending balances at the morning exchanges and settling these balances the same day by orders on the clearing house. This practice was a unique feature of the Boston clearing system and became an important part of the clearing arrangements. Before adoption of the practice, debtor banks that found their balances at the morning exchanges too large for convenient settlement with cash but who could easily call in the necessary amount later in the day, sent their representatives through the streets to borrow from neighboring banks. Because of the inconvenience and risk involved, the officers of the banks began to meet at the clearing house, and then, after the exchanges had taken place, to borrow and loan their balances. At one time some 60 percent of total balances were settled in that way. The rate of interest on these loans corresponded very closely with the rate on call loans — one of the principal methods of adjusting operating positions.

The Federal Funds market has experienced two distinct periods of development — the 1920's and the 1950's. Its development of the 1950's carried into the 1960's, confirming and sharpening the structural outline of the market and increasing the dimensions. A change in the functional role of the market between these two periods prevents strict comparisons.

Throughout the 1920's, banks participated in Funds trading almost exclusively as a method of adjusting reserve positions. While retaining this original function in the 1950's, Funds acquired increased importance both as an outlet for short-term investment of secondary reserves and, directly or indirectly, in connection with Government securities dealer financing. In the 1960's as well, an increasing number of banks sought Funds to support loans and investments.

After World War II, the practice evolved of making payment in Funds for an increasing number and variety of financial transactions. This practice was developed initially by banks when trading with dealers in U.S. Government securities. Funds payment provided banks with immediate adjustment in reserve position or portfolio arrangement. It subsequently became more convenient for the dealer to finance by the same method. Later, other customers of dealers and banks demanded settlement in Funds because it shortened the turnaround time and, consequently, the loss of interest between the sale and effective date of the new purchase by the investor.

Similarly, as business corporate structures became more fully integrated, financial officers developed methods of speeding the proceeds of collections from local and regional banks to those in major financial centers for disbursement or investment. There are now plans for automatic daily remittance in Federal Funds to the major money market banks of all balances in excess of a certain amount held outside the principal money centers.

Trading or exchanging Funds is today a more important part of the complex of interbank relationships which ties the units in the American structure into a system and provides an efficient means of distributing the volume of excess reserves according to need. Other settlements in Funds have moved financial markets toward unity in payment and away from the use of clearing house funds.

BEGINNINGS OF THE FUNDS MARKET

The Federal Funds market originated in New York City. The first trades were made among several of the leading city banks in the early summer of 1921.

In the late spring and early summer of 1921, depressed conditions had a diverse effect on the large New York City banks. While some of these member banks found that their reserves at the Federal Reserve Bank of New York had risen to considerable proportions, others were borrowing at the discount window. Banks with surplus funds had trouble finding outlets for reinvestment in the usual channels. Activity in the money market diminished, and open market money rates declined steadily from a 1920 peak, finally falling close to or below the average discount rate in all Federal Reserve districts after mid-1921.

This situation was discussed informally by several leading banks. As a result, the banks that were borrowing from the Reserve bank began purchasing the balances of those reporting excess reserves. These dealings involved the transfer of reserve balances on the books of the New York Reserve Bank from the reserve account of the lending bank to that of the borrowing bank, generally by an exchange of checks. In the beginning, it was the practice for both the lender and borrower to make their checks payable immediately. But to forestall the possibility of an early deposit of the borrower's check, it became customary for the borrowing bank to draw the check on itself, payable through the clearing house the next business day.[1]

In this way, the bank with excess reserves was able to realize a return on these reserves until they could be placed in loans, investments, or other outlets in the money market; and the bank with insufficient reserves was able to reduce its borrowing at the Federal Reserve bank. The banks also found that by buying Funds they avoided the trouble and expense of assembling collateral of customers' paper eligible for discount and of arranging a loan at the Reserve bank.

By mid-1923, a fairly active market in Funds had developed which the city banks used frequently in adjusting reserves among themselves. A few of the banks, however, did not participate until

---

[1]Officers' checks may no longer be used to return Funds to the selling bank by the buyer. Transfers are now made by entries on the books of the Reserve banks. See Board of Governors' Ruling, April, 1970, Appendix A and the discussion in Appendix B.

later in the period as a matter of policy. Nor did the Federal Reserve Bank of New York encourage the development of the market. It was argued that in contrast to Funds transactions, which affect reserves immediately, settlement in clearing house money enabled the Open Market Committee of the Reserve banks to take account of the net effect of transactions entering clearings. The Committee could thus make a better estimate of the factors affecting the volume of reserves of the money center banks the next day. As the decade of the 1920's progressed, trading within New York City broadened, and interdistrict trading of Funds on a limited scale developed. Before 1925, local markets also appeared in such cities as Boston, Philadelphia, Chicago, and San Francisco.

The typical block of Funds traded in the 1920's was $1 million, but blocks of $500 thousand appeared frequently — smaller blocks of $100 thousand were not uncommon in the early years and at various times since then when the market was tight. Although the typical unit traded is still $1 million, with the growth of correspondent bank trading arrangements, transactions as small as $50,000 have been common.

During the first year of the market, the volume traded rarely exceeded $20 million a day. Until 1925, the volume traded on an average day ran between $40 and $80 million. Trades were arranged by a succession of telephone calls from one bank to another. No facilities existed, as they do presently, for centralized market information.

From about 1925 on, normal daily trading increased further and ranged upward from $100 million, reaching $250 million at times during the latter part of the 1920's. The volume tended to approach the upper limit of the range on reserve settlement days[1] in New York because the greatest demand arose from banks making last minute adjustments in their reserve positions. Some 30 to 40 banks and 8 or 10 acceptance dealers accounted for most of the trading. Agencies of foreign banks located in New York were also important sources of Funds at times.

[1]Reserve settlement days were Friday until January 3, 1928, and Tuesdays and Fridays until March 19, 1942. Since then, settlement day has been Wednesday.

ROLE OF THE ACCEPTANCE HOUSES IN THE 1920'S

Although the member banks in New York City were the first buyers or sellers of Funds, the market of the 1920's and 1930's was brought to its full development largely by the discount or acceptance houses in the course of their normal operations. Some of these firms conducted business in U.S. Government securities, commercial paper, acceptances, and other investments. Moreover, the Federal Reserve System during the 1920's conducted a substantial volume of open market operations in acceptances as well as in Government securities. Transactions in acceptances were primarily used to meet seasonal variation in reserve needs, while transactions in U.S. Government securities generally were used to effect major credit policy shifts. The substantial part of these market transactions was with the discount houses, although the Reserve banks would buy properly endorsed acceptances from member banks when they were offered.

From about 1924 on, the System dealt with a list of recognized dealers — about 10 in number — when buying acceptances or Government securities for policy purposes or for the accounts of its foreign correspondents. Such recognized dealers were also permitted to sell acceptances and Government securities to the System under repurchase agreements. The Federal Reserve Bank of New York, because of its location in the Nation's financial center, accounted for the largest proportion of both outright purchases and transactions under resale agreements. When they conducted transactions in acceptances within their district, several other acceptance houses were recognized by one or more of the Federal Reserve banks. Those dealers in acceptances whose own endorsements were not approved by the Reserve System purchased endorsements from recognized dealers or from banks.

At least one of the leading acceptance houses maintained a nonmember clearing account at the Federal Reserve Bank of New York, as did several American foreign banking corporations that were active in the acceptance market. These accounts had been opened as early as 1919, partly as a convenience to the New York Reserve Bank in handling transactions in acceptances and Government securities. Thus, having these accounts, the firms were in a position to sell their own checks on the Reserve bank. In some cases, the deposit accounts of these firms were built up through sales of acceptances or

Government securities outright or under repurchase agreements to the New York Reserve Bank. In other cases, the acceptance houses and those firms which dealt in acceptances or Government securities, in settling transactions with the New York and other Reserve banks, acquired title to Reserve bank Funds before such Funds reached the commercial banks. In addition to their transactions with the Federal Reserve banks, dealers acquired title to Funds from several other sources: outright purchases and conversion of balances in excess of the customary balance carried with their commercial bank; proceeds of the sale of acceptances or securities to out-of-town banks received through the Reserve bank; payments received in redemption of U.S. Government securities and interest coupons; and maturing acceptances.

The dealers used Funds partly in settling their own transactions and partly in trading them. In the former case, Funds were used as payment for acceptances and U.S. Government securities when the terms so specified, as payment of calls on war loan deposits (predecessor of today's tax and loan accounts) where such accounts were maintained, and as payment for U.S. Government securities when payment was not made by war loan account. Alternatively, surplus Funds were sold in the market, and if there was insufficient demand, the balance was deposited in the New York Clearing House banks.

Funds deposited by a dealer in his regular account at a commercial bank drew only the rate then paid on demand deposits. However, when the dealers requested Funds in making withdrawals from their accounts, the commercial banks, if under pressure, charged them the call loan rate or more, depending upon their reserve position. On the other hand, a bank with a surplus of Funds might be willing to supply the dealer with its check on the Reserve bank at the discount rate or lower. Gradually the acceptance dealers began to shop the banks for Funds and found that regular purchases and sales could be accomplished. The leading dealers eventually developed a systematic daily telephone canvass of possible buyers and sellers in the market, collecting information about the demand and supply of Funds. They soon began to buy and sell Funds on a quarter-point spread. Later, as interdistrict trading developed, the spread ran as high as one percentage point at times because of discount rate differentials between the East Coast and West Coast.

7

The dealers usually purchased only small amounts of Funds outright but customarily acquired large blocks on an option basis for short periods. They also performed the service of combining small purchases into usual size trading blocks and at times would split large blocks for retailing.

MONEY BROKERS

As the market grew, some banks and several of the money brokers became market factors. The brokers found that the status of a bank's reserve position was important in relation to the call money market. The brokers viewed a lending bank with excess reserves as having "good money" — money which would be available overnight and could be used to reduce day loans, security deliveries, and overhead burden. Therefore, the brokers arranged to supply Funds daily for those banks with insufficient reserves, securing them from banks running an excess. The brokers considered this service an important adjunct to their call money operations since it led to procurement of blocks of call and time money on which they received a commission from the borrower. One of these firms was Faber, Garvin and Company — forerunner of The Garvin Bantel Corp.,[1] currently one of the four Federal Funds brokers in the market.

AREAS OF MARKET DEVELOPMENT

The acceptance houses and those American foreign banking corporations having branches in principal cities — particularly Chicago, Boston, Philadelphia, Cleveland, and San Francisco — developed a considerable volume of interdistrict trading and formed the focal point for local markets in some of these cities. In the late 1920's, a fairly active market had developed which was centered in Boston and included the larger banks in several major cities in central New England. Local markets in the 1920's were generally limited to those areas where financial activity was most concentrated. Atlanta, Dallas, Minneapolis, Richmond, and St. Louis reported only small

---

[1]The corporate title was adopted on June 1, 1966. The firm was previously known as Garvin, Bantel & Co.

amounts of trading among local banks. Some of these cities, however, at times supplied Funds to New York, Philadelphia, and San Francisco.

As might be expected, the New York City market for Funds was the largest both in terms of volume and in the number of banks participating. Trading consisted, for the most part, of transactions between city buyers and sellers and, to a lesser extent, of transactions between city banks and out-of-town institutions. In contrast to the 1950's and 1960's, bank size in most financial centers outside New York tended to be more nearly equal, and the banks that traded Funds were able to match off needs locally to a considerable extent. If excess Funds remained, they were offered to New York or to other cities. However, during the 1920's, certain New York City banks pursued a policy of not dealing in Funds with out-of-town correspondents and thereby discouraged the extension of the market. For these reasons then, the volume of interdistrict trading in the Nation was relatively smaller than at present, while the volume of intracity trading in the leading financial centers was substantially larger. The Funds market of this period was essentially local or regional in character.

The differentials in discount rates between most Federal Reserve districts which characterized the 1920's encouraged trading across district lines. During the late 1920's, an active interdistrict market developed with the West Coast. Advantages in supplying this market were found not only in discount rate differentials between certain eastern points and the Coast but also in time zone differentials. When New York banks closed at 3 p.m., San Francisco banks were still open for business since it was only noon on the Coast. This enabled eastern banks to estimate Funds in excess or deficit of legally required reserves and, if in excess, to sell balances in the West before the wires closed in the East about 2:30 p.m. Reaching the Coast about noon, Funds trading commenced immediately for the purpose of adjusting reserves. The Funds were usually returned to the East early the following day. The amount of excess Funds offered depended not only on time differences but also on correspondent relationships. For example, two large San Francisco branch banks depended on their wholly-owned eastern affiliates as important sources of Funds. These affiliates acted as agents for procuring Funds when they had no excess of their own.

Certain San Francisco banks solicited Funds from banks in many parts of the country and stood ready to receive them, up to certain limits, at all times and without notice, the agreements as to rates being understood. Under one such agreement, Coast banks received Funds if sent but did not pay for them except at the demand deposit rate, unless they could actually profit by their use. Others did not solicit or encourage forwarding of balances but would accept limited amounts. Since much of the trading in San Francisco was at agreed rates, or at the best price available, rates there bore little relationship to the Funds rate in New York City. In general, Federal Funds were received from most large cities in the United States — New York, Boston, and Philadelphia supplied the bulk, followed by Chicago, Detroit, Atlanta, New Orleans, St. Louis, Kansas City, and Dallas. In other cases, eastern Funds were sent to banks in the Midwest and forwarded from there to San Francisco. Funds from Dallas were frequently transferred to Los Angeles and thence to San Francisco through correspondents.

RELATIONSHIP OF FUNDS TO OTHER MARKETS IN THE 1920'S

The Federal Funds market of the 1920's was probably developed to the fullest extent possible within the framework of financial institutions of the period. Although it was an important market, the volume of Funds passing through it was small compared with either present volume or other sections of the money market in the 1920's. This position of the Funds market is explained in part by the narrower function it performed in the 1920's compared with today.

The short-term money market had come to include four principal markets centered in New York City — call and time loans on the Stock Exchange (generally called brokers' loans), commercial paper, bankers' acceptances, and U.S. Government securities. The New York banks placed funds for the interior banks in these markets but continued to hold some funds on deposit. During the 1920's, there was a marked increase in the investments made in brokers' loans for the account of outside banks by their correspondents. This practice became quite significant after 1924 when the volume of liquid funds available for investment was plentiful and the volume of commercial paper, the customary outlet for outside banks, was declining. City banks followed the tradition of placing funds for correspondents before their own.

Call loans, which accounted for about three-quarters of brokers' loans during the 1920's, were considered among the safest and most liquid available use for temporary surplus funds of banks and others. The call loan market also normally commanded higher rates than those paid on demand deposits — generally the New York City banks paid only 2 percent on these. Interior banks shifted from balances with New York City correspondents to brokers' loans, and vice versa, depending largely on the call loan rate. That portion of call loans which depended upon bankers' balances varied and represented the marginal supply of funds and thus linked the call loan rate closely with reserves of the city banks. Interbank balances, although relatively less important than earlier, became more and more a channel through which investments were made.

The several divisions of the short-term money market were well integrated and highly competitive. Fluctuations of any one rate usually caused sympathetic response in the other short-term rates, and the rates in the several markets generally changed in the same direction with a trend toward more uniformity. Competition existed to a greater extent among lenders than borrowers because lenders, principally the banks, operated in all of the markets, entering and withdrawing in the process of adjusting their money positions in response to operating needs in meeting customer demands. They moved from one market to another on the basis of both preference for and yield of particular money market assets at any given time. These shifting investor preferences were important in connecting the markets. The borrowers, on the other hand, represented distinct groups which did not have the same freedom of movement because they were generally more limited by peculiar or particular needs.

Table I shows the amounts of the various instruments outstanding in the money market during typical years in the 1920's and outlines the changes which occurred during the period. In addition to its dominance, the call loan market was the most centralized since loans were arranged through the money desk of the Stock Exchange. The commercial paper market, however, continued to be broadest during most of the period because it was used by the

11

greatest number of banks, accounting for 90 percent or more of purchases of the paper offered by the dealers. As noted, the operations of the System Account were conducted in the acceptance and Government securities markets. Consequently, the commercial banks considered these investments major liquidity instruments.

TABLE I
MONEY MARKET INSTRUMENTS 1922, 1925, 1928

Approximate Amounts Outstanding in Millions of Dollars (Partly Estimated)			
	1922	**1925**	**1928**
Brokers' Loans	$1,000-1,600	$2,000-3,000	$3,900-5,100
Call	800-1,200	1,400-2,100	3,510-3,980
Time	200-400	600-900	390-1,120
Bankers' Balances			
(Due to banks by			
N.Y.C. banks)	800-940	1,100-1,200	800-1,200
Commercial Paper	600-800	600-800	480-525
Acceptances	500-600	600-800	1,100-1,284
U.S. Government			
Short-term Securities	1,000-1,216	2,500-3,000	2,500-3,000
Federal Funds Purchases			
(Average daily volume)	40-70	100-175	100-250

SOURCES: *Federal Reserve Bulletin* and *Banking and Monetary Statistics,* Board of Governors of the Federal Reserve System and *Annual Report of the Secretary of the Treasury* for the years indicated. Federal Funds were reported in interviews with retired bank officials.

The chief function of the Funds market was refining the reserve adjustment process of the unit banking system, thereby effecting mobilization of reserves for more continuous use in the money market or for customers' loans at the bank counter. It improved the fluidity of the money market by bringing demand and supply into more rapid adjustment. Beyond this, Funds were used at times in settling security and other transactions by banks' customers. The Funds market was used as an important investment medium by relatively few of the banks. Alternative markets were generally more profitable, offering a wider range of choice with a good distribution of the volume of paper in each market. Funds today provide a substitute for several classes of money market instruments available in the 1920's and early 1930's.

RATE RELATIONSHIPS IN THE 1920'S

The Funds rate during most of the 1920's and the early 1930's tended to be limited by the discount rate. In comparison with other money market rates, the rate was more sensitive and tended to anticipate changes in bank reserve positions and factors affecting them because the use of Funds offered an alternative to borrowing at the Reserve banks. When the call loan rate was close to the discount rate in New York City, the interior banks with surplus Funds usually sold them in the Funds market to avoid the fee charged by correspondents in placing call loans, a fee that ranged as high as one-half of 1 percent. At other times, the banks used the Funds market as a last minute emergency outlet in placing surplus Funds not needed as reserves or loaned on call.

Funds were usually traded during the 1920's on a quarter-point spread, and even in periods of temporary ease, transactions did not take place on one-eighth of a percentage point spread. This was accomplished at times, however, by compromise — sale of same-size blocks at different rates, for example, one block at 3½ percent and the other at 3¾ percent. The rate generally kept in touch with the discount rate and the lower limit was determined to considerable extent by the rate paid on demand balances. The dealers would not sell at rates below those paid on balances by the commercial banks.

The Funds rate and the call rate at times tended to fluctuate in opposite directions, particularly when rising call rates attracted Funds over Reserve System wires from areas outside New York City, thus creating a surplus in the city. At other times, when Funds were demanded in the interior and call rates were low, the demand for Funds drove the rate up on occasion above the discount rate. Regardless of other factors, the Funds rate tended to be strong on many reserve settlement days.

CHART I
THE RATE ON FEDERAL FUNDS - NEW YORK

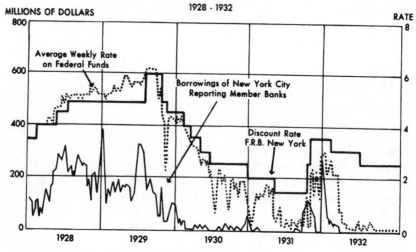

1928 - 1932

MILLIONS OF DOLLARS   RATE

Average Weekly Rate on Federal Funds

Borrowings of New York City Reporting Member Banks

Discount Rate F.R.B. New York

SOURCE: *N.Y. Herald Tribune* and Federal Reserve Bank of New York. Funds rate data not available in series form prior to April, 1928.

During 1928 and 1929, the Funds rate frequently stood above the discount rate, reaching a spread of three-quarters of 1 percent to 1 percent at times. Certain banks lacked eligible paper for rediscount while others that were lending heavily on call loans preferred to secure reserves in the Funds market rather than risk criticism at the Reserve bank by borrowing. After the panic of October, 1929, the Funds rate dropped sharply, partly because of the heavy inflow of Funds over Reserve System wires to New York to meet margin calls. Except for the period in late 1931 and early 1932 — when discount rates were raised because of the crisis abroad resulting in suspension of gold payments by Britain — institution of an easy money policy and gold inflows caused the rate on Funds to drop as low as one-quarter to one-eighth of 1 percent with some frequency in both these years.

THE MARKET IN THE 1930'S AND WORLD WAR II

The Funds market dried up during the Great Depression. Banks became very cautious about arranging trades because of the uncertainty of each other's condition. Many banks adopted the policy of operating with large cash cushions. The volume of trading began to decline, particularly on an interdistrict basis, as the rate of bank failures increased. Sporadic trading, however, continued in those cases where correspondent relationships were strong, and sometimes Government securities were pledged if a series of trades was contemplated.

Later in the 1930's, as loans fell and gold moved in volume to the United States from abroad, banks accumulated huge excess reserves (particularly from 1934 to 1937), and there were practically no occasions when there were borrowers in need. Toward the close of the 1930's, moderate trading was resumed on occasion. Increases in required reserves ordered by the Federal Reserve System in 1936 and 1937 and expanding loan and investment portfolios absorbed some of the overhang of excess reserves.

Early in 1941, as markets began to tighten in response to financial pressures resulting from World War II, Funds trading became more frequent, principally in New York but also in several other large cities. At least one money broker stood ready to provide facilities for matching the demand and supply of Funds in New York City. Volumes traded were small relative to those of the last half of the 1920's but larger than in the 1930's, probably averaging $75 to $125 million a day. The volume tended to increase toward the close of the war. Many banks ran excess reserve positions. The market, however, continued to be local or regional in character throughout the war years.

During the war, U.S. Government security prices were "pegged," resulting in a yield curve which rose from three-eighths of 1 percent for Treasury bills to 2½ percent for the longest term bonds. The lower end of the curve was established April 30, 1942, when the Reserve banks announced they would purchase all Treasury bills offered at three-eighths of 1 percent. In August, the Federal Open Market Committee instructed the Reserve banks to replace such purchases with sales of a like amount of Treasury bills with the same maturity at the same rate of discount, if requested by the seller before maturity. Consequently, the banks made most of their reserve adjustments through "puts and calls" on Treasury bills rather than in the Funds market.

SOME DIFFERENCES IN THE MARKET IN THE 1950'S AND 1960'S[1]

Today it is common practice for banks to offer excess Funds to, or secure Funds directly from, New York or other cities. Changes in operating policies with correspondents of many New York banks and the facilities for matching the demand and supply of Funds offered by the Funds brokers and by "accommodating banks" in various cities support this practice and make the market national in scope. As late as 1967, about one-half of all Funds transactions originated in or were accomplished through New York City. San Francisco and Chicago followed in trading volume, each accounting for about 15 to 18 percent of total Funds activity. During the last two years, however, as regional trading arrangements expanded, New York's relative position declined and the city's banks now account for between 35 and 40 percent of trading. Chicago's and San Francisco's relative positions have become more important, accounting for 17 to 20 percent of gross purchases.

Size differences between banks in one city, as well as distinct contrasts — local, regional, and national — in the character of various

[1]During the postwar period the Federal Reserve has collected data on Federal Funds transactions on several occasions. In 1955, the Federal Reserve Bank of New York began collecting data on daily purchases and sales by the large New York City banks.

Late in 1956, the System conducted a one-month survey of Funds transactions from major banks in each district. Some Federal Reserve banks collected historical data where available.

A three-year survey of Funds transactions at about 250 banks was carried out by the Federal Reserve beginning in September, 1959. Transactions included all loans and borrowings by banks for which payment was made in Funds. (See Dorothy M. Nichols, *Trading in Federal Funds—Findings of a Three-Year Survey*, Board of Governors of the Federal Reserve System, Washington, D. C., September, 1965.)

The 46 bank series was inititated by the System in 1964. This series comprises 8 New York City banks, 5 Chicago banks, and 33 other banks, and emphasizes interbank trades. (See "New Series on Federal Funds," *Federal Reserve Bulletin*, August, 1964, pp. 944-53.)

Data for gross sales and purchases of Funds have been reported for member and nonmember insured banks on Call Reports as separate asset and liability items since December 31, 1965.

Most Federal Reserve banks during the last two years have been collecting daily data on Funds transactions from all member banks. Definitions of Funds may differ from district to district, including or omitting repurchase agreements, and time periods may differ.

Beginning in July, 1969, the Weekly Reporting Banks report Funds purchased and sold on Wednesdays. The captions include repurchase agreements (see *Federal Reserve Bulletin*, August, 1969, pp. 642-46).

Data used in discussions in this booklet draw on all these sources. Many observers think that representativeness of the 46 bank series has diminished in the last two years as the market underwent rapid expansion.

banks' loan business, result in payment flows which prohibit complete adjustment locally. Similarly, intercity trading within most districts occurs in greater volume currently because of the more rapid growth of banks outside the traditional money centers and because a different pattern of financial settlement developed as these banks extended the scope of their activities. The highest proportion of intradistrict trading occurs on the Pacific Coast and accounts on the average for about a third of that district's Funds activity.

The late 1950's and 1960's witnessed further change in trading patterns and market structure. The development of trading within regions centered in large correspondents, while related to such trading in the 1920's, has distinct differences. Trading is more extensive and generally conducted at a uniform national rate. It involves a larger number of banks, and trading units are as small as $50,000 and sometimes lower. This kind of trading pattern has developed to meet the competition offered in regional market areas by the large central money market banks.

Perhaps more importantly it reflects competition among larger banks in interior parts of the United States to improve the flexibility of their own reserve positions, thus helping to retain and improve their position in influence and size. Competition among the regional banks, soliciting business over wider areas than previously, forced local competitors to establish facilities for their own correspondents.[1]

The post-World War II Funds market, in contrast to that of the late 1920's, developed without nonbank intermediaries quoting a spread in rates. Nonmember clearing accounts at Reserve banks, which were extended to several dealers in the earlier period, are no longer available. Thus, these nonbanks do not have the same access to facilities which would make dealing possible. Beyond this, the present market reflects the identity of reciprocal needs to the buying and selling bank along with wider and more continuous bank participation and the rapid and inclusive wire transfer systems for transmission of balances. The Funds broker through whom trades

---

[1] For example, Funds trading by the large Dallas banks in 1965-66 forced city banks in Oklahoma to offer trading services to country banks more willingly, and this resulted in extensive trading by Oklahoma banks.

may be arranged now is usually compensated for his service in indirect ways, the accommodating banks facilitate their own operations, and the bank which deals directly with another bank enjoys a mutual advantage.

Until the recent periods of severe credit restraint, many of the larger banks that deal on both sides of the market generally accomplished transactions at the same rate. During 1969, a number of these banks bought Funds at the bid rate and, after covering their basic deficiency in reserves, sold Funds to correspondents at the offering rate; usually this spread was one-eighth to one-quarter of 1 percent. At times when market rates developed rapid changes, the spread widened to one-half percent or more to protect against loss. Smaller city banks in regional centers that buy Funds from correspondents and pass on amounts not needed, however, usually operated on a spread of one-half percent. Their transactions are in relatively small units, and the banks are not in the market as continuously as the larger ones and therefore are exposed to a greater risk in rate fluctuation.

Currently, some banks at times "follow the clock," buying or selling Funds successively in New York and Chicago, occasionally in St. Louis or Kansas City, and finally in San Francisco or Los Angeles. Interdistrict trading is no longer influenced by differentials in Federal Reserve bank discount rates, except for very short periods caused by the normal lag as each of the Reserve banks acts to change its rate. The movement of the preponderant share of short-term Funds through a national market in effect precludes anything more than temporary differentials among districts. Trading "westward" has become significant for Mountain Time banks and those in contiguous territory in the Central Time Zone. Although these banks use the eastern market, an excess or deficit in the reserve position of a Dallas, Denver, or Phoenix bank can be corrected by transactions with the San Francisco district after the eastern banks are closed. Even Dallas at times makes as much as 40 percent or more of its purchases from San Francisco. The prevalence of branch banking on the Coast has facilitated Funds trading through fewer but larger banking systems with central management of money positions. The district is frequently a net supplier to other regions.

As was true in the 1920's, the core of the market is still the large banks, but today there are a greater number (between 60 and

70), and they are more widely distributed over the Nation. In addition, the market over the last 10 years has become characterized by a substantial number of relatively smaller banks which participate actively in interbank transactions on an unsecured basis. Even banks whose capital and surplus were not of sufficient size to enable them to undertake unsecured transactions were brought into the market occasionally in the 1950's through the use of techniques using several forms of collateral.

Funds transactions are important to a larger number of banks, and the volume traded continues to grow. At the same time, the banking system is better integrated. Its population is about one-half that of the 1920's, and the typical unit is larger in size. Funds transactions are considered by many observers as one of the effective instruments in redistributing reserve funds and in helping to effect greater uniformity of credit conditions throughout the Nation. Along with discounting, Funds transactions supplement reserve averaging. Efficient and more intensive utilization of available Funds permits the money market to function on a minimum of excess reserves and helps make the banking system more responsive to the credit control measures of the System.

FUNDS MARKET AFTER WORLD WAR II

The changes which developed in the banking system as a result of the Great Depression — easy money conditions during most of the 1930's, legislation, financing of World War II, and the increase of bank mergers and branch systems — provided a different structural setting for the money market when the postwar period opened. The rapid growth of production and population expanded the demand for banking services, while the growth in the size of business units created a demand for bigger banks and large capital accounts to permit an increase in the size of individual loans.

The rise in population and incomes and significant shifts in their distribution within the economy began to exert a marked impact on the pattern of bank assets. The greater diffusion of deposits throughout the United States, shrinkage of business borrowing in the form of commercial paper, decline in acceptance volume, and the tremendous growth of the market for U.S. Government securities altered the character of the money market. The market shifts, as well as legislation, brought the call loan market to an end before the formal closing of the money desk on the Exchange in 1946. These changes inevitably resulted in new money market arrangements, and in the new setting, the Funds market began to develop a strong national character.

Legislation which interacted on this situation included the Banking Acts of 1933 and 1935. The prohibition of member banks' role as agents for nonbank lenders in the placement of security loans, as well as the suspension of interest payments on demand deposits by the Banking Act of 1933 and the establishment of margin requirements under the Securities Exchange Act of 1934, were some of the important features of this legislation.

As the postwar period progressed, a more fully integrated structure of markets and institutions emerged. Financial institutions — both banks and nonbanks — became more closely interconnected. Mechanical arrangements for communication and the transfer of money market instruments followed rapid technological advance. Correspondent relationships among the banks were broadened and increased in scope. Specialization developed further to meet the particular needs of various lenders and borrowers, and transactions are now effected rapidly and at low cost. Knowledge of markets became more widely diffused, and linkage between the short-term money market and the long-term capital market strengthened as more financial and nonfinancial institutions began to conduct transactions in more than one market. Thus, influences operating in one market or affecting a group of institutions, have tended to be transmitted more rapidly to other related markets, or a group of institutions, with the result that differentials in rates substantially diminished. To the extent that regional markets remain, they have become more closely tied to the national market centered in New York.

The significant increase in size, marked change in composition, and the broadening and shifting ownership made the marketable portion of public debt a new sensitive medium for adjusting cash positions of financial institutions and others. The marketable debt also came to serve as a more permanent and continuing investment outlet. The development of Reserve System credit policy in the postwar period was reflected in higher rates for Government securities and a greater reliance on borrowing for reserve adjustment by individual banks. Bank reserves ultimately were placed under pressure.

With the increase in breadth and activity in the Government securities market as short-term rates rose, the competitive search for Funds became more intense. Government security dealers found it necessary to become active participants in the Funds market both as intermediaries and, in some instances, as principals. Dealers' securities transactions to a great extent have always been settled in Funds, but insistence by customers on this form of settlement made a substantial addition to demands.

All transactions between New York dealers and out-of-town customers are completed in Funds. Until early 1969, however, transactions within New York or other local areas involving maturities of one year or more were settled in clearing house funds. These trades in all maturities in both round and odd lots are now settled in Funds. Moreover, negotiation over the form of settlement (clearing house money or Funds) has become a factor in most financial transactions. Money market instruments — bankers' acceptances, commercial paper, certificates of deposit, as well as new long-term corporate and municipal capital issues — usually specify payment in Funds.

DEVELOPMENT OF THE REPURCHASE AGREEMENT BY GOVERNMENT SECURITIES DEALERS

Before World War II, the nonbank Government securities dealers borrowed to finance their positions largely from New York City banks, and the proceeds were almost without exception in clearing house money. [1] This continued to be the general situation during the period of relatively easy money from soon after World War II until 1952. New York banks were again a major source of dealer financing during the 1954 and 1958 periods of monetary ease.

---

[1] Dealer banks financed their position through allocation of "own bank funds" to dealer departments.

During these periods, the rates that the bank charged the dealers ran, as a rule, above the yields on short-dated securities and above the discount rate — except when credit was quite "easy." Nevertheless, the dealers could generally accomplish profitable "carries" because yields on the intermediate and longer term securities were higher.

During restrictive phases of System policy (1953, 1955-1957, and 1959), dealers in Governments frequently found difficulty in obtaining adequate financing from the New York City banks at rates corresponding to yields on securities in their inventories. Charges to dealers by the major banks fluctuated from 3½ and 3¾ to 4 percent. Very few U.S. Government securities carried rates as high as 3¼ and 3⅝ percent. As a consequence, the dealers sought financing outside the city with a yield margin in their favor.[1] A variety of business corporations, state treasurers, and widely scattered banks were already investors, and dealers encouraged many of these investors to become lenders through repurchase agreements or "buy back"[2] transactions as an alternative to direct investments in securities.

The proceeds on repurchase transactions are available in Funds, in contrast to dealer loans by New York City banks which, until the early 1960's, were largely in clearing house money and required conversion to Funds. Also, the net cost to the dealer is generally lower than at the bank counter, and adequate amounts of credit are more dependable, particularly as participation by nonbanks and banks has widened. New York City banks do not make repurchase agreements with nonbank dealers because these agreements carry a lower rate than can be obtained from dealer loans.

---

[1] See *A Study of the Dealer Market for Federal Government Securities,* Joint Economic Committee, 1960, pp. 87-89, and *Treasury-Federal Reserve Study of the Government Securities Market,* Vol. II, 1959, 120-21, for discussion of costs of dealer borrowing in the 1950's; and Louise Freeman, "The Financing of Government Security Dealers," *Monthly Review,* Federal Reserve Bank of New York, June, 1964, pp. 110-15, for a discussion of costs in the 1960's.

[2] Commercial banks used repurchases in interbank borrowing to a considerable extent in the old national banking system. As noted previously, the repurchase agreement was also used in the acceptance and U.S. Government securities market during the 1920's. In the 1950's and 1960's, the instrument was adapted to a new setting, and its current use reflects such refinements as automatic renewal of agreement, lending at flat prices, and automatic adjustment of rates to the market. Securities used in repurchase agreements are mostly U.S. Governments. They may, however, be mixed—certificates of deposit, securities issued by U.S. Government agencies, and acceptances.

CHART II
BORROWINGS OF NONBANK DEALERS AND DEALER
LOANS BY NEW YORK CITY BANKS

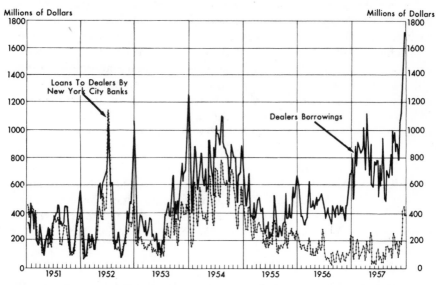

SOURCE: Borrowings of nonbank dealers based on information supplied by sample of
nonbank dealers. Dealer loans by New York City banks are from weekly
condition reports. Data are for last Wednesday in the month.

The rate on repurchase agreements is determined by money market conditions at the time of negotiation. It is principally related to the rate on Funds, dealer loans, and to a lesser extent, Treasury bills. Availability of collateral may also be a determinant. Until the tight money of the last two years, the repurchase agreement made for overnight commonly carried a rate slightly above the Funds rate but below the dealer loan rate.

During the tight money market of 1969, however, dealers at times were able to make repurchases with certain nonbanks at a level below the Funds rate, usually at or just below the rate on commercial paper. A complex of factors accounted for this development. Among them were shortage of collateral or desire to conserve holdings of U.S. securities on the part of banks, dealer willingness and need to carry inventory, and investor convenience. Whether the transaction was initiated by the investor or the dealer also influenced the rate. Repurchases made for a longer term than overnight may

23

carry a rate below the Funds rate — how much will depend on the degree of tightness or ease in the market and the outlook for rates.

One large dealer began developing repurchase agreements as early as 1948, and the practice was slowly followed by others. As early as 1955, a leading dealer interested in the development of repurchases had 105 accounts including 77 banks and 15 large non-financial corporations. The balance was distributed among insurance companies, savings banks, and funds of state treasurers. These accounts were scattered through 57 cities in 38 states, and the volume for the year aggregated $36.5 billion, an average of $100 million a day. This was 88 percent of this dealer's total financing.

The development of sources of financing outside New York was virtually completed early in the 1960's, and since then the proportion of Funds secured from sources other than the New York City banks has tended to stabilize. Even the dealer banks in recent years have used repurchases to finance a substantial part of their dealer positions.

This development of new sources of financing reflected the changing structure of the postwar money market — the passage from one with an overhang of surplus reserves to one of relative reserve scarcity in which reserve use carried increasing premiums of costs.

Also, a new generation of officials in charge of corporate treasuries and in bank and dealer money positions — stimulated by larger cash flows, rising interest rates, and other costs — established imaginative new relationships, thus breaking tradition.

Since 1960, New York City banks have become more liberal in making call loans to nonbank dealers, particularly when markets have been relatively easy. Responding to competition with the outside banks and nonbanks, they began to make a substantial proportion of the loan proceeds available in Funds. Beginning in 1965, the total of these proceeds was generally made available in Funds. Their competitive positions improved moderately as reflected in a narrowing of the spread between the dealer loan rate and the repurchase rate when compared with earlier periods. Narrowing of the spread was caused chiefly by a tendency for the rate on repurchases to increase relative to other rates as the instrument became more widely used. Except in

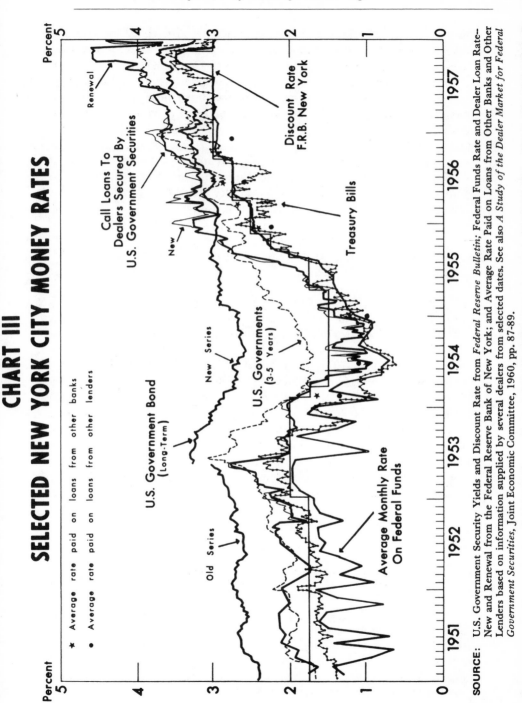

CHART III
SELECTED NEW YORK CITY MONEY RATES

★ Average rate paid on loans from other banks

● Average rate paid on loans from other lenders

Renewal

Call Loans To
Dealers Secured By
U.S. Government Securities

New

U.S. Government Bond
(Long-Term)

New Series

U.S. Governments
(3-5 Years)

Old Series

Average Monthly Rate
On Federal Funds

Discount Rate
F.R.B. New York

Treasury Bills

Percent

0   1   2   3   4   5

1951   1952   1953   1954   1955   1956   1957

SOURCE: U.S. Government Security Yields and Discount Rate from *Federal Reserve Bulletin;* Federal Funds Rate and Dealer Loan Rate–
New and Renewal from the Federal Reserve Bank of New York; and Average Rate Paid on Loans from Other Banks and Other
Lenders based on information supplied by several dealers from selected dates. See also *A Study of the Dealer Market for Federal
Government Securities,* Joint Economic Committee, 1960, pp. 87-89.

periods of strain, the New York banks account for about a quarter of dealer financing[1] — a significant share, and moderately more than presently supplied by banks outside New York. Dealers, however, continue to view New York banks as a marginal source of Funds. The rates are almost always the highest for both new money and renewals, ranging generally one-quarter to three-quarters of 1 percent above the Funds rate.

The repurchase allows a lender to invest without the risk of fluctuating security prices and to tailor maturities to his needs. At times, the repurchase may include a larger amount than a comparable issue of specific maturity or term. The investor can thus make full employment of available money up to the date when it must be used for other purposes. The rates may be somewhat lower than yields on most alternative short-term investments, but the advantages cited offset this.

The nonbanks enter into repurchases with security dealers for varying periods running as long as several months[2] and still supply about one-half of dealer financing. To the financial officers of these organizations, the collected portion — good money — of their commercial bank account is considered available in Funds. Thus, they request their bank to pay Funds to the dealer against delivery of U.S. Government securities to be held in custody.[3] Although most of the Funds involved are used to finance dealers' inventories of U.S. Government securities, even the longer term financing arrangements have a definite effect on the trading market. The Funds come from the banks' position and may cause them to leave the market on the supply side or enter on the demand side on the particular day on which the transaction occurs. The dealers, on the other hand, at

---

[1]See Louise Freeman, *op. cit.*, pp. 107-08, for a discussion of amounts of dealer financing from various sources. See also *Report of the Joint Treasury-Federal Reserve Study of the U.S. Government Securities Market*, Washington, D. C., April, 1969.

[2]Long-term repurchase agreements (16 days or more) are viewed by many dealers as sales of securities out of their inventory, since the contract matures usually only a day or two before the maturity of the security.

[3]A transfer of bank balances that is accomplished by entries on the books of a Reserve bank in the reserve account of a member bank and is available on the same day is a Funds transactions. Thus, Funds are in effect sold to dealers.

times have a balance which is offered for sale. Although these transactions are usually quite moderate in size, they have some influence on the trading market.

It should also be noted that from time to time in order to ease conditions in the money market or increase availability of reserves, the manager of the System Open Market Account at the Federal Reserve Bank of New York may make repurchase agreements with nonbank dealers against Treasury and Federal agency securities and bankers' acceptances usually at the discount rate.[1] They are generally made for overnight or 2 or 3 days but at most within 15 days. These transactions aid in financing dealers and supplement open market operations. Repurchases are not made with bank dealers because they have access to a greater variety of financing sources than do nonbank dealers.[2]

To improve flexibility of its operations, the Open Market Account Desk introduced the matched sale-purchase-contract in July, 1966, as a means of absorbing reserves temporarily or for a varying period of time (normally one to seven days). These transactions consist of sales by the Desk of specific issues of Treasury bills at a specified price for cash delivery and simultaneously a commitment to purchase the same bills for later delivery. In contrast to repurchases these agreements are made with both bank and nonbank dealers. The transactions may be used to affect the Funds rate with little or no impact on the Treasury bill rate.

FUNDS TRANSACTIONS BY BANKS

Banks most frequently employ their Funds on a short-term basis by making direct, unsecured sales to other banks. These transactions are flanked by several varieties of secured transactions including common forms of repurchases. The great bulk of interbank trades, however, are for overnight and are unsecured.

---

[1]Transactions have been made at rates above and below the discount rate. In the late 1950's and early 1960's, the System made repurchases at less than the discount rate, generally at the Treasury bill rate. In recent years, some purchases have been made above the discount rate when money market rates were higher than the discount rate.

[2]Such sources include the Federal Reserve discount window, direct participation in the Funds market, and payment for some new Treasury issues with tax and loan account credit.

Until the Comptroller's ruling in June, 1963,[1] which freed transactions by national banks from lending and borrowing limits, secured transactions, when used, were generally considered a function of the size of either the seller or the buyer, or both. Secured transactions permitted exemption from the lending and borrowing limits of the National Bank Act and continue to do so for state member banks where corresponding rulings have not been made by state banking commissioners or by statutes. The collateral involved — some form of collateral loan agreement or repurchase — usually represented the most conveneient mechanical arrangement, although for some borrowers credit standing was a factor.

Secured transactions in interbank trades are more generally a characteristic of trades between banks outside New York, although they are often used by outside banks when selling to New York, and on occasion, when borrowing. While there has been some decrease in the volume of secured transactions since the Comptroller's ruling, banks continue to observe the broad limits and rules in dealing with one another which have been part of the practice of the market. Banks similarly continue to appraise each other's credit standing, and collateral is still frequently required of smaller banks and as a matter of policy in other cases. More emphasis may be placed on collateral if certain banks want to exceed previously agreed limits.

A number of banks in large centers have found that purchases of Funds offer a partial substitute for the demand deposit balances which they acquired in the 1920's when interest payments on these balances were permitted. They have come to use substantial amounts of Funds in their operating positions. The pattern of trading varies among the banks; some accommodate others, both buying and selling the same day; some are net sellers or net buyers; and others run balanced positions. On the selling side, the Funds market now significantly fills the position formerly occupied by the old call loan market as a secondary reserve investment market. Many banks which previously adjusted their positions in Treasury bills now largely use Funds transactions. The market has also become a major source of financing for Government securities dealers. Banks in principal cities throughout the Nation now frequently supply more dealer financing through overnight repurchase agreements than banks in New York and Chicago — historically the largest source of dealer borrowing.

[1]See Appendix A for more detail.

THE FUNDS RATE

Funds transactions between banks are now quoted in terms of the effective rate or prevailing rate — the level at which the great bulk of transactions are accomplished. The quote is considered representative of the entire market, New York City and elsewhere. During most of the postwar period the quotes have usually changed by one-quarter of a percentage point; more recently (since late 1962), as in other markets, the quote change has frequently been one-eighth of a percentage point, reflecting the increased breadth of competition within this market and in relation to alternative markets. Quotes of one-quarter of a percentage point were also typical in the 1920's.

During most of the 1920's and the postwar period, the Funds rate generally fluctuated between the discount rate and a lower limit of one-half or one-eighth of 1 percent — a point where most banks can recover costs. This reflected a close association of member bank borrowing from the Federal Reserve and the discount rate, which was generally in touch with market rates. Thus, having access to the discount window at the Reserve bank, member banks were usually unwilling to pay more than the discount rate for Funds.[1]

Over a substantial period in 1928 and 1929 (see Chart I) and since March, 1965, the Funds rate has almost continuously been above the discount rate. The premium bid on many days in the 1920's reached spreads ranging between one-eighth of a percent and 1¼ percent above the discount rate. Willingness to pay this premium was attributed to lack of eligible paper and fear of criticism by the Reserve bank because of the large portfolios of loans to the stock market held by member banks.

The premium bid in the mid-1960's developed initially from the efforts of several of the New York City banks to secure a larger volume of reserves for lending and investing as well as the fear of

---

[1]Market observers, however, reported several instances in 1959 and one in May and one in early August, 1964, where one-eighth of 1 percent more than the discount rate was paid. In October, 1964, and during the rest of the fall, the Funds brokers reported some transactions in size on a number of trading days at one-eighth of 1 percent premium. The effective rate, however, did not exceed the discount rate.

Reserve bank criticism if their borrowings from the Federal Reserve were used for extended or continuous periods to support extensions of credit. Other reasons for premium rates included a shortage of Government security collateral to serve as the basis for advances at the Reserve bank and awkwardness in the use of eligible paper.

CHART IV
RATE ON FEDERAL FUNDS AND FEDERAL RESERVE BANK OF NEW YORK DISCOUNT RATE

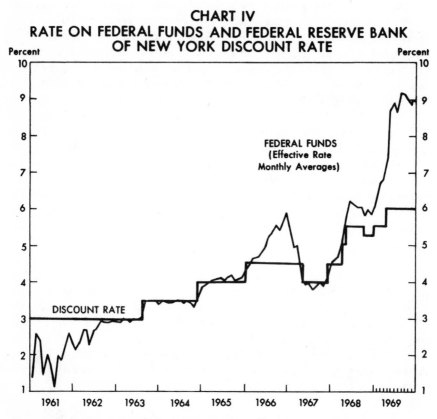

SOURCE: Federal Reserve Bank of New York.

From March, 1965, to the present time, the effective Funds rate has almost continuously been above the discount rate. The increasing size of the premiums developed from exceptionally strong bids by the larger banks as their loan and investment volume expanded in response to customer demand. During this period, the discount rate was used sparingly and lost touch with market rates particularly when they were rising during the restrictive policies in 1966 and 1969. The Federal Reserve Board was reluctant to approve or initiate increases in the discount rate. It was feared, among other things, that the "announcement effect" of even a modest change might be exaggerated and thus stimulate still higher levels of market rates.[1] The premium at times was 2 to 3 percentage points. In a sense, the Funds rate became a discount rate. Discipline exercised at the window, however, insured that the Federal Reserve advances were not a steady and continuous source of supply for any given bank.[2]

This development reflected the changed attitude of the banks which had come to view purchases of Funds as one of the primary sources for covering deficits in cash flows or rebuilding excess reserves and sales as a principal secondary reserve asset. It also reflected the widespread acceptance of liability management by banks to gain liquidity by varying liabilities instead of assets. In this context, certificates of deposit, Euro-dollars, and bank related commercial paper were increasingly relied upon. Payment of a rate for Funds by the large banks competitive with other market rates made the Funds market quite dependable even in periods of credit restraint.

Banks continued to pay a premium for Funds as System policy gradually eased during 1970. The size of the premium decreased, however, and by October the Funds rate was closely aligned with the discount rate. The premium amounted to about one-eighth to one-quarter of 1 percent on the average. Volume traded remained high.

---

[1] *Annual Report* of the Board of Governors of the Federal Reserve System, 1966, pp. 94-96; 1969, pp. 70, 77.

[2] The relative level of the Funds rate and the discount rate does have some influence on borrowing at the Reserve banks. A differential of a full point or more between the two rates may encourage the banks to seek the cheaper discount accommodation. Under these conditions, it is expected that administration of the discount window would be more searching. The impact on borrowings of differentials in these rates is less certain if they are no more than one-half of 1 percent. Country banks' decisions of whether to buy Funds or borrow at the Reserve banks are typically more sensitive to smaller rate margins than the city banks. It should be noted that borrowings in the Funds market are not identical with those from the discount window since in the latter case they must meet purpose constraints as outlined in Regulation A. Banks, however, whose borrowings meet such purposes may make their reserve adjustments by using the cheaper source—the discount window. It is not expected that a bank will routinely use the window as just one of several alternative sources of funds such as Euro-dollars or CD's, thereby exploiting the rate differential.

SOME FACTORS INFLUENCING THE FUNDS RATE

During the credit squeeze in 1966[1] and the period of intensive credit restraint in 1969, banks showed a strong preference for the Funds market in making reserve adjustments. This was a factor contributing to increases in the rate on transactions and the volume of Funds traded. The intensity of demand was reflected in the increasing spread of the Funds rate above the discount rate. In fact, the preference for Funds over borrowing at the window has continued to the present time.

Paying more than the discount rate for Funds reflects the elasticity of the demand for them. The market may be said to represent a marginal demand and supply schedule in which increases of demand and supply quickly result in changed rates — in contrast to some other markets where competition is less perfect. The Funds rate acts as a sensitive indicator of shifting pressures in the banking system, particularly when related to who is supplying the Funds, the volume of the flows, and the depth of the demand. The huge flow of Funds during the last five years and widespread participation of both city and country banks of all sizes underscore this characterization of the market.

Currently, Funds are bought and sold by banks at several points in each Federal Reserve district. Each local selling point is a market, but New York City still predominates as the central market. About half the transactions originate in or move through New York City, and the brokers and principal accommodating banks are located there.

Local selling points are intimately connected with the central market and with one another. They are "linked" in the sense that price differences can bring transactions from one market to another, and some of the competing buyers and competing sellers complete transactions in more than one market within a district or in several districts. In a real sense the market is national.

---

[1]A letter from the Federal Reserve System dated September 1, 1966, requesting the cooperation of member banks in curtailing loans to business, stated that member banks experiencing deposit losses would be extended credit for a longer period than usual if they made efforts to slow loan growth instead of cutting further into holdings of securities, especially municipals. The banks did not take advantage of the offer to any extent.

CHART V
DAILY RATE FOR FEDERAL FUNDS AND FEDERAL RESERVE BANK OF NEW YORK DISCOUNT RATE, 1969

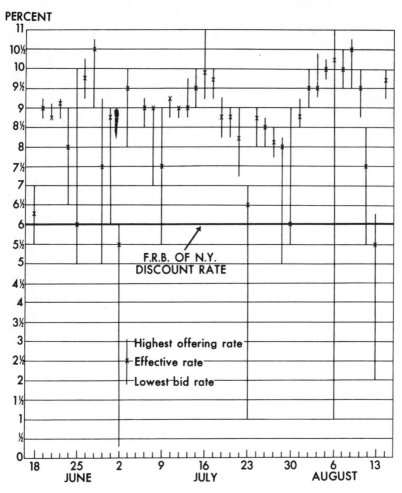

SOURCE: Federal Reserve Bank of New York.

Transactions are accomplished rapidly and at low cost in increasing volume for increasing numbers of banks at *nearly* uniform rates. This reflects a high degree of adjustment between demand and supply and price and quantity exchanged. In each local market, the same general forces determine the rate which may exist at any given time, although the magnitude of these forces may vary from market to market.

These rates are not unrelated to each other but are distinct prices, and the departures from the effective rate merely indicate a range of quotations on a given day.[1] Lack of perfect adjustment and a uniform rate arise from institutional friction, absence of complete knowledge of the market as a whole, and use of Federal Funds by nonbanks and others.

The growth in unity and breadth and the increase in efficiency of the Federal Funds market during the 1960's have strengthened the connections between the various divisions of the money market and between those of the money market and the longer term credit markets. A given volume of Federal Funds now moves through the market with less change in rates than before, and market participants may move back and forth from one sector of the money market to another in response to shifting rate differentials without causing disruptive price changes.

Although longer run influences, such as shifts in System policy, affect the Funds rate, it is also influenced by a shift of reserves among money market and country banks and the ebb and flow resulting from banking and other financial transactions. A persistent tendency for the rate to rise indicates a greater demand for reserves relative to supply, and a persistent tendency for the rate to fall suggests a smaller demand relative to the supply of reserves. Aside from temporary problems arising from the geographical distribution of reserves, distribution among money market banks, or unusual short-term demands, such as Treasury financing, the Funds rate shows a consistent and generally stable relationship to net borrowed reserves. Longer run shifts in the relationship, however, may occur under certain conditions. The Funds rate has risen relative to net

---

[1] See Chapter 4 by Dorothy M. Nichols, *op. cit.*, for a detailed discussion of determination of rates and rate structure. This study provides a detailed analysis of Funds transactions by about 250 banks that reported to the System between September, 1959, and September, 1963.

borrowed reserves when deposit drains become cumulatively large and bank liquidity becomes strained. The credit squeeze in 1966 and the intense credit restraint in 1969 are cases in point. Demand for Funds to make reserve adjustments increases under these circumstances. The Funds rate during much of the postwar period has been considered a key variable, along with net borrowed reserves, by the Open Market Account in maintaining the desired money market conditions.

As a general rule, the Funds rate shows quite a distinct weekly pattern. The rate tends to be firmer on Thursdays and Fridays and to soften on Tuesdays and Wednesdays. The softening is usually most pronounced on Wednesday, the last day of the statement week. This change within the week reflects the operating practices of institutions in the market, such as those followed by different banks in determining their reserve positions. Some buyers and sellers come to the market at different times. Firmness on Thursday and Friday reflects the opening of the reserve week for all member banks. Thursday is the payment day for weekly Treasury bills, and banks most active in financing the dealers absorb Funds. Many banks usually like to develop a cushion of excess reserves which can be drawn down later in the period to meet shifts in deposits or other pressures. The position must also be established for the weekend on Friday, since these transactions carry over until Monday.

The softness of rates at the end of the statement week principally reflects lessened demand factors. Available data do not show that supplies of Funds are larger on those days. In the opinion of most market observers, lessening of demand may be attributable to several factors.

Reserve requirements have been satisfied and those country banks which do not trade Funds shift excesses to city correspondents frequently. The widening use of Funds during recent years has caused country banks to compute requirements more accurately and sell excesses to city banks. When these flows from country to city banks coincide with periods of sufficiencies for Reserve city banks, the market tends to fade away.

Efforts have been made to adjust for anticipated volumes. Some banks have sold estimated excesses, and others have bought to cover estimated deficiencies a day or two prior to settlement dates. The results, however, have not always matched expectations.[1]

It should be noted that excess Funds may appear with resulting downward pressure on rates during periods of scarcity. This has happened occasionally in the past if member banks borrow in excess of their needs prior to a long weekend or when float or other operating factors produce sizable amounts of Funds in excess of estimates.

MONEY MARKET INSTRUMENTS 1950-1969 AND SOME FUNDS RELATIONSHIPS

Chart VI traces the continuous growth and change which have occurred during the postwar period in the composition of money market instruments. This change reflects an effort to improve the flexibility of the various institutions within the market itself and to maximize the usefulness of the existing volume of money market funds in making final adjustment between demand and supply of credit. Special techniques have been developed by both borrowers and lenders which facilitate flows between markets. Knowledge of the market also has become more widespread and internal diversity reduced, particularly since the mid-1950's.

Business corporations have become important suppliers and users of money market funds, both directly and indirectly. The activity of nonbank participants has increased partly because interest is no longer paid on demand deposits. Deposits have been redistributed in the banking system to the extent that corporate treasurers have shifted from demand deposits to money market investments, and these treasurers have become increasingly active in shifting from one market to another. This activity has also been a

---

[1]See also the discussion of the effect of the introduction of and experience to date with the Lagged Accounting Reserve Plan on pp. 70—72. At the present time, the Open Market Committee is re-examining its own processes for agreeing on policy objectives and its strategy for accomplishing them. Monetary aggregates, such as the money supply and bank credit, are currently being given more weight. Emphasizing a quantitative target may result in more amplitude of fluctuation in the sensitive rates and net borrowed reserves from time to time than when money market conditions were used as a major policy objective.

factor in slowing deposit growth at the large money market banks and increasing the velocity of money. As all sectors of the market increased in competitiveness, the range of fluctuations in rates has been reduced except during the recent periods of severe monetary restraint. Considerable variability in money market conditions seems to inevitably accompany such a policy. In some markets in 1969, spread between bid and asked rates was frequently widened from the characteristic one-eighth percent, to one-quarter percent, and on occasion to three-eighths percent.

Maturing instruments in the several sectors of the money market are now generally paid off in Funds as opposed to clearing house checks. Currently, unless agreed otherwise, money market instruments bought and sold in the secondary market are usually deliverable in New York the next business day following the date of the transactions, and settlements are in Funds. Banks in New York and Chicago frequently act as issuing agent and alternate paying agent when such service is required to reduce deliveries and collection expense. Banks in other principal money centers may also perform these services. U.S. securities and the majority of Federal agency securities are payable at Federal Reserve banks.

Funds and Treasury Bill Markets

The Funds market and Treasury bill market are today the dominant sectors of the short-term money market and reflect business conducted for a widened variety of customers in substantially increased volume. Over two-thirds of all trading volume in U.S. securities in 1969 was conducted in Treasury bills. At the same time, Federal agency securities, up to two years in maturity, have become important in trading.

These are the markets in which the banks complete most of their reserve adjustments, and virtually all open market operations of the System Account are conducted in the U.S. Government securities market. These operations have an immediate impact on the supply of Funds and spread the effects of System monetary policy throughout the financial markets. Correspondingly, large money market banks and Government security dealers are the major participants other than the Federal Reserve. Because of different uses, the relative importance of each market to borrowers and lenders cannot be compared on the basis of absolute magnitudes.

Beyond the Funds and Treasury bill markets, other sections of the money market, some old and some new, are important not only for reserve adjustment but also for lodgement of short-term funds, and the participants link these markets to others. Some markets have changed in both function and character compared with past periods. An example of this is the brokers' loan market. Although these loans have shown a large increase in outstandings during the last several years, they are now of relatively small significance in adjusting bank reserve positions. The market is more generally used by the larger banks as a secondary reserve investment. As such, its character is considerably different from the 1920's, when working capital balances of corporations were placed in call and time loans to brokers through the agency of New York City banks.

Dealer Loans

The market in dealer loans with U.S. Government securities as collateral[1] developed during the postwar period, accompanying the rise in trading in Governments. It is highly specialized and closely related to both the Funds and Treasury bill markets. These loans are made on call or overnight by several of the leading New York City banks, and they help to balance out residual reserve needs in the money market as a whole.[2] In effect, the banks act as lenders of last resort for the Government security dealers. Daily volume may range from $100 million to over $1.5 billion.

This market has some aspects of a customer loan market in that most of the banks do not feel free to terminate loans without regard to the individual borrower's position. Generally the banks influence the volume of outstanding loans by making daily changes in the "posted" loan rates on new loans and renewals — announced each day after the bank has initially determined its reserve position. By varying their rates and administering the volume of loans within the

---

[1]Collateral may also include certificates of deposit, securities issued by U.S. Government agencies, acceptances, and commercial paper.

[2]One or two Chicago banks are also important sources of these loans.

framework of posted rates, these banks use dealer loans to adjust their reserve positions to reflect changes within the market itself as well as broader changes affecting the money market as a whole. Dealer loans are thus considered an important money market instrument for New York City banks.[1] The rates on the loans are established below the call rate on other security loans, but generally one-quarter to three-quarters of 1 percent above the Funds rate and frequently above the yield to dealers on the securities in their inventories.

Aside from the influence of normal operating factors, an atmosphere of ease or tightness in the general money market stems from the strength of the demand for Funds, the intensity of reserve use, bank reserve adjustments through net purchase or sale of Treasury bills, and the willingness of the banks to make dealer loans. Geographical distribution of reserves — whether concentrated in financial centers or country areas at any given time — may be a short-run underlying influence. In the final analysis, however, the degree of restraint or ease in the money market is reflected in the volume of member bank borrowing at the Reserve banks.

Commercial Paper

In the older markets, dealer commercial paper still serves a respectable cross section of industry. Along with the enlarged dollar volume of recent years, issuers have also increased, numbering about 500 in 1969. Although banks remain major purchasers, they now hold only one-third of outstandings. Nonfinancial corporations account for most of the balance. Agreements by the dealer to

---

[1]Some analysts view repurchase agreements made with dealers by banks outside New York as being more closely related to collateral loans than to interbank trades because a number of the outside banks feel an obligation to renew such agreements even if it necessitates borrowing Funds to support the loans. In other instances, the bank merely follows an impersonal attitude—makes the loan if it fits its reserve position because the rate frequently is fractionally higher than a Funds transaction. The loan is considered similar to a direct trade of Funds with another bank. The element of customer relationship in repurchases with banks outside New York is more likely to be found in the Midwest and West. Whether repurchases should be classified as collateral loans to dealers depends upon whether interest centers upon dealer accommodation or some other aspect of the market. In any event, there is an extremely close relationship between the direct Funds and collateral loan markets. Lines of distinction are not clear-cut. For further discussion of this point, see "New Series on Federal Funds," *op. cit.* This article also develops the concept of "basic reserve position" for 46 major Reserve city banks.

repurchase the paper from the buyer do not usually occur, but for good customers in an emergency, the dealer may try to resell the paper on a "best efforts basis."

More recent money market instruments include directly placed sales of finance company paper, and in early 1969, bank related commercial paper [1] began to grow in volume. This latter paper first appeared in small volume during the credit squeeze of 1966 and provided banks with an additional nondeposit source of Funds, enabling them to meet some of their loan demand. Both dealer and directly placed paper have maturities of three days to nine months with most carrying maturities of less than 90 days. The nine-month maximum maturity exempts commercial paper from registration with the Securities and Exchange Commission, and the exemption requires that the proceeds of these notes be used for "current transactions."

Sales finance company paper, first issued in some volume in the 1920's, was not handled by dealers and was ineligible at the Reserve bank discount windows. Only modest amounts were held by banks. The rise of finance companies to a predominant position in the market accompanied the growth of consumer credit. The credit record of the paper established it as prime quality, and by the late 1930's dealers began handling it. Dealers continue to place the paper of some finance companies, but most is now placed by the issuer. The expansion in economic activity after World War II forced finance companies to seek short-term credit in amounts beyond the ability or willingness of banks to service them either through direct lending or purchase.

The market for finance paper broadened to include nonfinancial corporate treasurers and a variety of other investors. Corporate treasurers currently account for close to 60 percent of the volume of purchases of this paper, and since the advent of the master note toward the end of the 1950's, it is estimated that bank trust departments have come to account for about 20 percent of the purchases. The master note is a device for pooling temporarily

---

[1] Bank related paper is commercial paper issued by bank holding companies, affiliates of bank holding companies, or affiliates of banks.

uninvested funds of a number of investors (typically the beneficiaries of trusts) under a single agreement. Bank holdings, on the other hand, are relatively small, accounting for less than 10 percent.

If need arises on the part of the buyer, the issuer of directly placed paper will generally repurchase the outstandings, often with rate adjustments, however. Since the close of the war, the dealer function—locating buyers and suiting terms to needs—has increasingly been performed by the finance companies.

About 85 percent of bank related paper outstanding has been placed directly with corporate customers, and the balance sold through dealers. All kinds of commercial paper have increased significantly in volume—fourfold—since 1965, reaching a peak of $40 billion in June, 1970. Excluding bank related paper, the market has recently supplied about 25 percent of the credit represented by the combined total of commercial loans at large banks and commercial paper.

The increase reflects the extreme tightness of bank credit in 1966 and 1969, attempts to rebuild corporate liquidity in 1967, and the congestion and high cost in the long-term capital market. A number of utility companies used the market until the time when short debt could be funded at lower rates. In addition, since 1963, when permission was granted, certain utilities have financed current needs and accounts receivable in the market. Of particular interest is the use made of the market by nonfinancial corporations during the last several years in supplementing internal sources of funds and in providing an alternative and supplement to bank lines of credit. The market expanded so rapidly and the demand for credit was so intense during recent years in an atmosphere of general euphoria that some paper did not receive the customary scrutiny as exemplified by the bankruptcy of the Penn Central Transportation Company in June, 1970. About $87 million of this paper sold through dealers and rated prime by the National Credit Office was held by investors.[1] Commercial paper, however, will undoubtedly remain a popular alternative to bank financing. The market will be influenced by quality preference and show more caution for anything other than top rated paper. Some decline in outstandings may result.

[1]*Wall Street Journal,* August 13, 1970, pp. 1, 16.

Aggressive banks used the market through their affiliates to help hold their competitive positions. Proceeds from the sale of commercial paper by a bank holding company, its affiliate, or a bank subsidiary were generally used to supply funds to the bank through the purchase of existing loans from the bank or to finance the activities of the affiliate or subsidiary, such as mortgage servicing or factoring. In this way, the bank could make new loans, thereby accommodating its customers, or pressure on the parent bank's resources was eased.[1]

A relatively small amount of the paper known as "documented discount notes" has also been used to accommodate customers and avoid pressure on the bank's resources. The bank customer's note is sold by the dealer accompanied by a guarantee or irrevocable letter of credit issued by the customer's bank.

Bank related commercial paper amounted to about $4.5 billion at the end of 1969. By midyear 1970, outstandings had increased further to a level a little over $7½ billion.[2] At this level it comprised a significant share of total commercial paper. Considering the

[1]In line with its restrictive credit policy, the Board of Governors proposed in October, 1969, that if the proceeds of the sale of bank holding company paper or that of one of its affiliates were used to supply funds to the bank, the sales would be subject to Regulation Q. At the same time, it ruled that such paper issued by subsidiaries of banks was already subject to Regulations Q and D. However, the Board suspended interest rate ceilings and waived reserve-requirement penalties on the later paper to the extent that volume did not exceed the amounts outstanding on October 29. As well, it took no final action on holding company paper.

Using the authority in the Act of December 23, 1969, the Board, in January, 1970, proposed a 10 percent reserve requirement for bank related paper. Subsequently, after further discussion, the Board announced on August 17, that effective September 17, 1970, a reserve requirement of 5 percent would be imposed on a member bank affiliate's paper with a maturity of 30 days or more. Maturities of less than 30 days would be subject to the requirements on demand deposits. The authority of the Reserve banks to waive penalties for deficiencies in reserves resulting from the issue of such paper by subsidiaries was withdrawn. Simultaneously, required reserves on all time deposits in excess of $5 million were reduced one percentage, effective on the same date. The combined action was expected to release about $350 million of reserves net. This result was suited to continued moderation of the System's restraint policy inaugurated at the beginning of the year. In June, the interest rate ceiling on CD's of 30-89 day maturities was suspended. Since most commercial paper is issued in denominations of $100 thousand or more, the imposition of reserve requirements on bank related paper places instruments of this kind on practically an equal basis in terms of reserves with negotiable CD's.

[2]This class of paper will decline in anticipation of reserves to be required against it.

commercial paper market as a whole, corporate treasurers have succeeded the banks as major paper buyers, and the market has cut substantially into the loan business of commercial banks with finance companies.

Businessmen's and finance companies' cost of borrowing in this market was less than at the bank counter, even at the advanced rates reached after 1965 after allowance was made for compensating balances. Similarly, bank holding companies and affiliates found it a cheaper source when measured against the cost of Euro-dollars and other nondeposit funds to their bank affiliates.[1]

Business and finance company commercial paper market borrowers feel that the market has provided them with an alternative source of funds which is usually easily accessible and offers both flexibility in amount and terms of borrowing as well as a dependable availability of funds.

During the first half of 1969, the banks also procured additional reserves by selling over $1 billion from their portfolios under repurchase agreements to corporate customers. Such repurchases were limited to transactions between banks by a Federal Reserve Board ruling on July 25, 1969.[2] Since that date, a repurchase made by a bank with a corporate customer can be made only with U.S. Government or agency securities as collateral.

Bankers' Acceptances

Since 1958, the volume of bankers' acceptances has almost quadrupled, reaching $5.5 billion at the end of 1969. This reflects increasing reliance of domestic importers and exporters on acceptances as well as the rise in financing of foreign storage and shipment of goods. Acceptances for these purposes account for about 50 and 40 percent of outstandings, respectively. It is estimated that about half of the borrowing for foreign storage and shipment is undertaken to

---

[1] See pages 94-98 for detail on the Euro-dollar market.

[2] The Board stated that the proceeds of such repurchase agreements were indistinguishable from deposit transactions except on a formalistic basis. See Appendix A for more detail.

finance Japanese trade with other nations. Acceptances are also used to cover domestic storage and shipment and to some extent to create dollar exchange. Acceptances for all purposes except dollar exchange may have maturities up to six months. Dollar exchange acceptances, however, are limited to a maturity of not more than three months.

The severe credit restraint in 1969 and the limiting effect of the Regulation Q ceiling even led some banks to create and sell "working capital" acceptances in order to continue their loan expansion. These acceptances were ineligible for purchase or discount by the Federal Reserve because they were not trade related. The volume did not exceed $200 million at year end, but by midsummer 1970, it was estimated to have doubled.

Trading in acceptances focuses on six dealers, four of whom also trade Government securities. This market has become somewhat broader than it was in the first half of the 1950's. In part, this broadening reflects both more acceptance financing by a larger number of banks and the increasing interest of corporate and institutional treasurers in all short-term investment outlets. Foreign buyers — both commercial and central banks — although important, are today less significant participants than formerly. Domestic commercial banks and large savings banks remain the major purchasers. In 1969, acceptance rates rose to record levels and became increasingly competitive with other short-term investments. Even the small denominated bill of less than $100 thousand, heretofore considered a nuisance, was easily sold and attracted institutional odd lot buyers and even individuals. Banks sold most of the "ineligible" acceptances to their customers in 1969, and in 1970, there was a limited amount of trading by one or two dealers.

In contrast to the 1920's, the market is now considerably larger in absolute size but much smaller and less important in relation to the total volumes of money market instruments. The Federal Reserve now buys only limited amounts of acceptances for its own account. Some banks continue the practice of holding their own bills for investment or accomplish transactions through dealers on a "swap" basis. Some banks sell to their correspondents and other customers from their own supply. At times, a bank will enter the market as an agent on behalf of its customers. Similarly, banks will bid for acceptances if the holder wishes to sell. These practices, however,

CHART VI
MONEY MARKET INSTRUMENTS 1950-1969
Approximate Amounts Outstanding (Billions of Dollars)

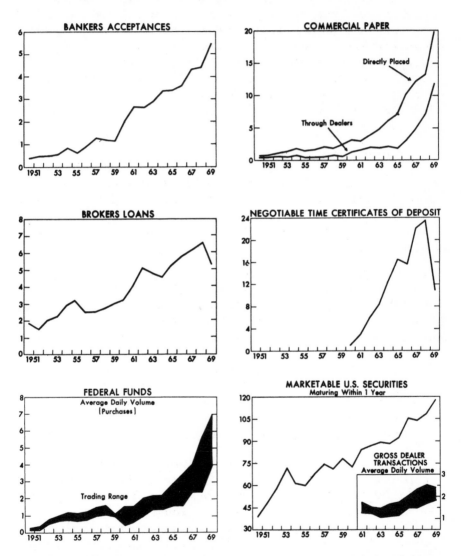

SOURCE: *Federal Reserve Bulletin* except Federal Funds. Funds data based on report of 250-275 banks September, 1959 — September, 1962, and 46 large banks since then. Data on Federal Funds and certificates of deposit partly estimated for some years. Brokers' loan data for 1969 are June 30. All other data are year-end figures.

appear to be decreasing or stabilizing, with more trading through dealers.

The acceptance market, along with the market for dealer and directly placed commercial paper, provides an important tie between the short-term money market and the bank counter. This occurs as borrowers switch from these markets to the bank counter in meeting needs. The prime rate on commercial loans has become an important part of the structure of money rates. Linkage with the long-term capital market is also provided through the bank counter as borrowers fund bank loans, depending in part upon the relationship of capital market rates to the prime rate.

Certificates of Deposit [1]

Although certificates of deposit have been issued in negotiable form for many years in parts of the Nation, they have become a significant money market instrument only since 1961. Earlier issuers did not expect their certificates to be traded. In fact,there was no organized secondary market.

In order to combat both the instability and shrinkage of their deposits which had been in process during the 1950's, the New York City banks announced that they would issue CD's to domestic business corporations, public bodies, and foreign sources. Issuance was expected to attract short-term corporate funds lodged elsewhere in the banking system and also provide an instrument to compete for corporate balances which were being invested in a variety of money market instruments, principally in Treasury bills. These CD's are usually issued in large denomination with minimum face value of $100,000, and maturities range from 30 days to one year or longer. Most maturities, however, are concentrated in the short-term area.

In late February, 1961, the First National City Bank of New York began to issue CD's. Two major innovations were introduced. The certificates were made negotiable, and the Discount Corporation of New York announced that it would make a market for certificates, thus broadening appeal. Competitive forces led banks in other centers to follow suit. Outstanding amounts have grown rapidly and include a variety of maturities but with considerable concentration in the short-term area.

[1] Negotiable CD's are issued and traded on yield to maturity basis.

Issuers are widespread geographically and by size of bank. Increases in outstandings have typically occurred during periods of relative ease or stability in the markets. Since rates paid are governed by Regulation Q, banks are forced to withdraw from the issue market as money market conditions firm, offering rates reach Regulation Q ceilings, and such ceilings remain unchanged. Under these conditions, market short-term rates rise relative to the Regulation's ceiling, and certificates become noncompetitive with other instruments. The rise of open market rates (not subject to the constraint of regulation) above — or their fall below — existing rate ceilings leads to the retardation or acceleration of issues as interest sensitive investors move to obtain the highest possible yields. As the market evolved, a number of the leading banks adopted the practice of varying the rate offered on certificates and, by this method, used certificates to adjust their reserve position.

Toward the end of 1968, a record high of $24 billion of outstandings was reported. Subsequently, the intensification of the System's restrictive credit policy which began to develop at the year end lifted market rates well above Regulation Q ceilings. Outstandings by the end of 1969 had dropped to about $10 billion because of net runoffs — about five times the size of the decline during the restrictive credit period in 1966. The move to a restrictive credit policy in the first half of 1969 was accompanied by a decision to leave Regulation Q ceilings on time deposits unchanged and thus below market rates. This was the first time that Regulation Q had been used by the Federal Reserve with the direct intention of restraining bank credit expansion. In 1966, market rates did not pierce the Regulation Q ceilings until midsummer, and the net runoff in CD's occurred in August and September toward the end of the restrictive period. The regulation was used at that time to supplement other policy instruments. The decision not to change time deposit rates and the reduced availability of bank reserves interacted on the demand for bank credit throughout the year in 1969, as it had after mid-1966. Banks were forced to seek nondeposit sources of funds — such as Euro-dollars and commercial paper — and to use the Funds market more intensively as a source of funds to accommodate customers' credit demands. Prior to 1966, Regulation Q ceilings were generally accommodated to market rates.

To the holder, at least of better known names, the secondary market, centered in the principal U.S. Government security dealers, provides reasonable liquidity except during periods of tight money, such as occurred in 1968 and 1969. The mere existence of the market has broadened the acceptance of all issues by facilitating sales to third parties before maturity for most certificates. Trading volume has ranged in "good markets" from $40 to $125 million daily average, while dealer positions have ranged from $150 to over $600 million. In "poor markets," such as occurred in 1966 and 1969, dealers substantially cut their positions, as supply and consequently trading volume dried up. In 1969, both the dealer positions and trading volume were nominal, falling as low as $1 to $2 million at times. Some distress selling occurred at times of sharp rate change.

The most active periods of the secondary market have occurred when dealers expected profits could be made. Until 1965, Regulation Q ceilings on the shorter maturities were somewhat below market rates for long periods, and the ceiling provided a cushion against market loss as holdings approached maturity. The yield curve descended as maturity shortened, permitting original holders to offer their CD's at lower rates (higher prices) than when acquired. In this way, they established a profit over and above the interest earned during the period held. With the establishment of a single rate for all maturities (December, 1965, to April, 1968), dealers acquired positions only when the rate outlook was stable or they expected rates to decline. They were exposed to undercutting, as issuers could make unexpected changes in rates. When the ceilings were raised in April, 1968, step rates based on maturities again provided a cushion against market loss when market rates were below ceilings, and for several months dealers were again able to acquire large positions on a favorable "carry" either with repurchases or dealer loans. By the end of the year, market rates and issue rates had climbed well above the ceilings and remained there throughout 1969, severely curtailing dealer activities.

Expansion of economic activity slowed during 1969, came to a halt near the year end, and declined during the first half of 1970. System policy accordingly became less restrictive, and moderate but progressive growth in the money supply and other financial aggregates was resumed. Reflecting these developments and as adjustment in business continued, pressures in the financial markets eased gradually as 1970 progressed. Short-term interest rates declined on balance as a consequence. In this context the Board of Governors liberalized the Regulation Q ceilings toward the end of January, raising the rates for each maturity. In June, the ceiling on the 30 to 89 day maturity range was suspended indefinitely, effective June 24. As a result of the January action, as market rates adjusted, banks were able to add CD's in moderate volume in the following months. The June action was undertaken partly in recognition of possible heavy demands on commercial banks for short-term credit resulting from uncertainties in the commercial paper market arising from the bankruptcy of the Penn Central Railroad Company and partly to support the easier credit policy. The System also used the discount window and open market operations to forestall liquidity pressures. Freed from the constraint of rate ceilings in this maturity, the banks aggressively sought short-term CD's to accommodate borrowers who could not obtain funds in the paper market. Banks received a substantial inflow of funds in response to offering rates of about 8 percent.

By late fall, the outstanding volume of CD's had reached $24 billion up from about $10 billion in early February. Dealers' inventories rose steadily and averaged over $400 million by the end of September. Trading in the secondary market became more active returning to earlier levels. Dealers were for the most part able to finance their inventories at favorable "carries" largely on the basis of Federal Funds.

The June action is the first suspension of the rate ceiling which has occurred. If ceilings should eventually be discarded, the rate paid by individual banks offering CD's would become increasingly a function of the average rate prevailing in the market, the volume of CD's outstanding, and the amount of new issues proposed. This development could lead to a more even flow of marketing of issues and better balance of factors in the secondary market.

As a short-term investment, certificates of deposit compete principally with three-month Treasury bills and commercial paper, both dealer and directly placed. They are held mainly by corporations and other businesses, although state and local governments and foreign entities also hold significant amounts. Generally, banks do not frequently buy other banks' certificates. Unlike other money market instruments, variation in amounts of CD's outstanding may influence the reserve position of banks because of the lower reserve required for time deposits. Issuing rates reflect the increased competitiveness of the CD's with other sectors of the money market. As the market has developed, changes in issuing rates have declined from one-quarter of 1 percent to one-eighth of 1 percent.

Other Market Instruments

Strong competition in the money market, charcteristic of the past decade, was clearly reflected by the offering of straight, unsecured short-term notes by the First National Bank of Boston in early September, 1964. A dozen or more large banks scattered over the Nation followed suit. These notes were directly placed by issuers in multiples of $1 million at rates that competed with finance company paper, negotiable CD's, and other money market instruments. A limited trading market centered with major U.S. security dealers subsequently developed. Only about $600 million of these notes were outstanding at any one time. In contrast to the CD's, they required no reserves or insurance and were not subject to rate and maturity restrictions imposed by Regulation Q. On the other hand, the issuance utilized some of the bank's capacity to borrow. Effective September 1, 1966, however, bank issues of short-term notes of less than 2 years in maturity were brought within the provision of Regulations D and Q, being defined as deposits in the interests of equity.

The variety of competition and money market participants' willingness to try to improve the flexibility of the institutions within the market itself have also been reflected in the issuance of short-term notes by the Federal National Mortgage Association inaugurated in April, 1960. In the private sector, the Savings Bank Trust Company also began issues of short-term notes in October, 1962

The FNMA notes are issued at a discount and are unsecured, with maturities designated by lenders ranging from 30 to 270 days with a wide choice of denominations. The FNMA has placed increasing reliance on these notes, and along with the Federal Home Loan Bank, has during the last three years increased the number of issues with maturities up to 2 years. This use of Federal agencies as intermediaries has provided significant amounts of money for the real estate mortgage market. The Savings Bank Trust Company has an issue of three year notes outstanding, and both these and its short-term securities are largely secured by FHA and VA real estate mortgages. Like the Federal agencies, the Trust Company uses a dealer in placing its notes. The outstanding volume of the Trust Company notes, however, is relatively small as are the amounts which are likely to be issued.

STRUCTURE OF THE MARKET AND INTERBANK TRADING

The Federal Funds market is primarily an interbank market.[1] In the early 1960's, on an average day about $3.5 to $4 billion of Funds was shifted from bank to bank, but on many days in the latter part of the 1960's, the total probably averaged close to $10 billion and fell to $3 to $4 billion only on occasion. These transactions[2] represent more than a fivefold increase in the volume since the late 1950's These are gross figures and include some double counting which occurs as funds are shifted from ultimate suppliers to final users.

On the average, only about 10 percent of total activity is with other than a commercial bank—chiefly U.S. Government security dealers, savings banks,[3] and corporations. At times, however,

---

[1]The discussion in this section emphasizes interbank trades of Funds. References are made, however, to transactions between banks and nonbanks. Many banks use these transactions for the same purpose as interbank trades. Effective February, 1970, the Board of Governors narrowed the category of Funds transactions permitted member banks by bringing within the coverage of Regulations D and Q such transactions "with any person other than a bank and its subsidiaries, various governmental institutions, or a securities dealer in certain cases." The term bank was also defined. See Appendix A, pages 103-04.

[2]Available data for member banks classifying transactions as purchases and sales generally show an excess of purchases over sales. This reflects transactions with nonbanks and nonmember banks and a number of small banks for which reports are not currently available.

[3]Legislation particularly in New York (April, 1969) and Massachusetts (August, 1969) permitting or clarifying the authority of savings banks to make unsecured sales of Funds resulted in a considerable increase in their activity. Savings and loan associations also make use of the market but frequently with repurchase agreements. Cooperative banks in Massachusetts since February, 1970, may make unsecured transactions.

transactions with these institutions may comprise as much as a quarter of total transactions.[1] Member banks, however, are always involved as a buyer, seller, or intermediary.

Some 350 member banks[2] are presently regular participants in the market, buying and selling Funds on from one to several occasions in almost every reserve period. These banks hold about 60 percent of total commercial bank deposits and include practically all banks with $100 million or more of deposits. The most active participants are found in Reserve cities, but some 60 to 70 larger country banks have substantial regular dealings, and another 400 trade less frequently — perhaps as often as 25 times a year. Estimates place the total number of participants as high as 3,500 banks, more than double the number five years ago. Many of these banks will have only several transactions at one time or another during the year and include those that range down to less than $1 million in deposit size. Usually the transactions of the smaller banks are sales made possible by excess reserves arising from seasonal or temporary forces.

[1]Nonbank dealers generally clear their securities transactions through one or more banks, and the clearing banks maintain a record of Funds paid out for, or received on account of, the dealer's transactions. These Funds frequently approximate $100 to $200 million per day and are charged and credited to the dealer at the going rate. Settlement is made periodically—weekly or monthly—on a net basis. One large dealer, however, still performs his own clearing in everything except Treasury bills and short-term Federal agencies and acquires and disposes of some Funds directly.

On the average over a period of time, a balance will generally prevail between the amount of Funds that a nonbank dealer may have had to pay for securities (or to repay a Funds loan) and the amount of Funds that he has received on the sale of securities (or from a Funds loan). If any large discrepancy arising from differences in the Funds rate exists at the end of an accounting period, the expense borne by the bank on account of Funds payments is settled between the bank and the dealer. Because of this, dealers seek to capitalize on excesses of Funds which they may have at particular times in order to offset some later charge by their clearing bank. Such transactions in Funds are accomplished only among the New York City banks and are not included in the interbank trading figures.

[2]A number of the larger nonmember banks and the agencies of foreign banks are frequently important sources of Funds. They sell excess balances in member bank correspondent accounts as Funds. The sales may be made to third banks with appropriate entries in the member banks' deposit accounts at the Reserve banks, but in many cases the transaction is accomplished on the member bank's own books by transfers from the deposit account to "money borrowed" or similar account on their own books. Currently the agencies restrict most of their sales to New York City banks. Frequently the agencies will sell Funds through repurchase agreements with Government securities dealers.

TABLE II

PURCHASES OF INTERBANK FEDERAL FUNDS

Period	Number of banks	Daily-average gross purchases (in millions of dollars)*
1925-32	30-40	100-250
1951-53	75-100	350-450
1955-57	125-200	800-1,200
1960-63	175-275	1,500-2,000
1963-66	180-350	2,000-3,500
1966-70	225-400	3,500-9,000

*Amounts are partially estimated and approximate and include only active traders. Lower limits refer to earlier parts of designated periods. Based principally on the "46 Bank Series" beginning in 1960.

The Reserve city banks as a group, as well as the large country banks, minimize excess reserves throughout the computation period. Others accumulate excess reserves and sell only toward the end of the period. Since the reduction in the size of the trading units in many accommodating banks' trading arrangements, however, more of the smaller country banks have begun trading continuously throughout the reserve period. Still others make a closely calculated use of borrowed Funds in carrying a basically overinvested position. The last practice has tended to assume increased importance for a number of large banks in recent years. Some of the smaller country banks, on the other hand, still do not customarily make full utilization of their excess reserves and as a group maintain sizable balances throughout the reserve period. In two midwestern districts where there are large numbers of very small banks, about half the number do not participate.

These differences in policy and in administration of assets, as well as variation in depth of market knowledge, account in large part for differences in trading patterns. Funds transactions are still affected by "rules" observed by correspondent systems which limit transactions outside the group. Some banks also will submit to brokers lists of other banks with which they will or will not trade.

This type of friction has diminished in recent years but is responsible in part for indirect routing of trades and occasional inelasticities.

Funds transactions began to grow in volume as well as in frequency in 1947 and 1948. This reflected the increasing pressures in the money market and the upward movement of interest rates as the banking system began to adjust to the postwar period. Interdistrict dealings in Funds with New York and other centers — which began to resume at the close of the war — increased slowly during the early postwar years and were handled almost entirely by correspondents. Further, the growth of the Funds market since the 1940's has been encouraged by Funds brokers, whose facilities form an important part of the national market.

Through the early 1950's, the structure of the market changed somewhat, shifting from a direct exchange of Funds between banks to an exchange through an intermediary or broker. The development of facilities for matching the demand and supply of Funds through a broker was accompanied by even faster growth in the activity of accommodating banks. At the same time, the market changed from one primarily regional and local to one strongly national in character, with its center in New York. With the growth of the accommodators outside New York since 1960 and the matching of transactions within correspondent groups, the national market now more largely clears the significant part of residual needs. The transactions are accomplished at minimum cost.

BROKERS AND ACCOMMODATING BANKS

Until December, 1958, when the Irving Trust Company established its Funds desk,[1] The Garvin Bantel Corp., a member of the New York Stock Exchange, was the only Funds broker in the market, and there were as few as 7 or 8 accommodating banks, most of them in New York City.

The Garvin Bantel Corp. initiated its interdistrict business in 1948 and encouraged the participation of out-of-town banks. This

---

[1] The Funds desk is run separately from Irving's transactions in Funds for its own account or accommodation of correspondent banks.

business began to become significant at the beginning of the 1950's as increasing numbers of banks began to direct transactions through the firm. Garvin Bantel estimates that close to 80 percent of total Funds traded were channeled through the firm until about 1953. With the expansion of the accommodating banks, this percentage dropped to 50 percent by 1957 and subsequently fell to about one-quarter to one-third. Since the entry of Mabon, Nugent and Co.,[1] also a member of the New York Stock Exchange, in the fall of 1963 and George Palumbo & Co., Inc., a money broker, in November, 1964, four firms have shared the market volume moving through brokers. The increased volume of transactions handled by brokers, shown in Table III, reflects new entrants since 1950, but more significantly it is the result of increased trading by the larger banks.

These firms act merely as agents in bringing buyers and sellers together through regular daily telephone contact with market participants. In addition, there are eight banks in New York City and another 30 or more commercial banks in other parts of the Nation — at least two in each of the Federal Reserve districts — that perform an accommodating business for correspondents. They differ from brokers in that they generally deal as principals and frequently trade on both sides of the market. These are the major accommodators, and during the last four years, some 40 more have offered this service in limited degree. The increase in the number of accommodators in the Midwest, Southwest, and West during the last 5 years was significant. With the exception of San Francisco and Chicago, most of the important accommodators are in New York, and, with the brokers, they form the largest focal point of the market. The accommodators outside these three cities generally service correspondents on a regional basis and may cross district lines to a limited extent.

The position of brokers in the market, however, has an importance beyond the volume figures. Various market participants use them as sources of information when seeking impersonal deals

---

[1]Before its merger with Nugent & Co. on February 15, 1965, Mabon & Co. conducted the Funds brokerage.

TABLE III

PURCHASES OF FEDERAL FUNDS
THROUGH BROKERS

Year	Number of Banks (Estimated)	Amounts (in millions of dollars)	
		Total	Daily Average
1949	15-20	$22,000	$100-150
1950	30-40	39,000	150-200
1951	35-45	53,000	210-250
1952	45-50	68,000	260-320
1953	50-75	70,000	280-340
1954	75-85	83,000	330-360
1955	85-100	79,000	320-350
1956	115-130	86,000	350-400
1957	130-145	87,000	310-340
1958	135-155	115,000	350-400
1959	140-160	94,000	330-360
1960	160-175	132,000	375-425
1961	180-210	158,000	450-510
1962	180-220	185,000	535-600
1963	185-225	160,000	430-540
1964	190-230	185,000	415-610
1965	200-240	281,000	650-887
1966	225-250	442,000	1,050-1,330
1967	230-255	465,000	1,155-1,400
1968	240-270	512,000	1,200-2,100
1969	240-275	816,000	1,700-2,800

SOURCE: Data 1949-1962 supplied by The Garvin Bantel Corp. — the only broker then in the market. Volume data 1963-1969 based on reports of three brokers to the Federal Reserve Bank of New York.

An accurate percentage of Funds transactions cleared through the brokers in relation to total activity cannot be computed because of double counting. Not only does the activity of the accommodating banks overstate the net movement of Funds from ultimate supplier to ultimate user within a given day, but the activity of the brokers will include some of the same transactions reported by the accommodators. Hence, in a movement of Funds from Bank X to Bank Y, two purchases may be reported — the purchase by the accommodating bank from Bank X and the purchase by Bank Y. They may be identical. The Funds may ultimately move to Y from the accommodating bank through one of the brokers.

with other banks as well as for general information about the market. The ability of the accommodating banks to serve their customer banks is also dependent, in part, on the service of brokers in facilitating contacts or furnishing information, particularly when the supply of Funds is fluid.

The brokers, along with the correspondent banks, play a significant role in bringing buyers and sellers together. As bids and offers of Funds begin coming in early in the morning, the brokers attempt to match them and establish an opening rate for the market. Each broker works independently but is aware of what the others are doing through information received indirectly. The opening rate established in New York is widely quoted as large banks and U.S. securities dealers call in to check the rate, and it tends to set the pattern for the rest of the country.

New entrants into the Funds market during the last few years include many relatively small banks whose correspondent relationships are close or who, for one reason or another, prefer not to deal through the brokers. In other cases, neither their unit transactions nor their volume is large enough to warrant participation in the money market except through their correspondents. A number of banks have also been encouraged to trade through regional accommodating arrangements.

Some accommodators — two-way trading banks — are net buyers, while others run balanced positions. Although all of the two-way traders are large banks, not all large banks conduct two-way trading. There are also differences in the use of the market within a given area, including New York. Thus many banks are referred to as adjusting banks, appearing as net buyers or net sellers or running a balanced position.

The variety of facilities for accomplishing Funds transactions is a product of the last 10 years. It reflects the growth of the market, heightened competition among large as well as many smaller banks, changes in practice and policies of participants, and more widely diffused knowledge of the market.

Since 1965, the greatest growth in participation has been among the banks in the $10 to $50 million deposit grouping. During the last two years, however, the participation rate of banks with less than

$10 million of deposits has increased substantially. In general, activity is related to bank size with the proportion of banks that trade increasing with each size class up to $50 million in deposits. As noted, the reduced size of the trading units in correspondent trading arrangements has not only encouraged small banks to enter but has increased the frequency of their trades. In recent years, the upward movement of interest rates and to a lesser extent rising costs led many banks to find it reasonable and logical to participate continuously in the Funds market even foregoing investments in other markets.

Country bank participation now includes about 60 to 95 percent of this class of member banks in a number of districts. Among these are New York, Philadelphia, Cleveland, Richmond, Boston, San Francisco, and Chicago. In the Minneapolis and Kansas City districts, the participation rate of the country banks, which was only about 20 percent as late as 1967, has increased significantly during the last several years. At least 45 to 50 percent of the country member banks were in the market at one time or another by the end of 1969 in these districts. The market now provides a way for all but the smallest banks to maintain a more fully invested position. Evidence shows, however, that a number of these banks are still unaware of the market and others have no desire to participate.

FUNDS TRADING PATTERNS[1]

Several of the largest accommodating banks — six in New York City and one on the West Coast — account at times for as much as 50 percent of total activity. They account for about one-half of gross purchases and 40 percent of sales. Their volume sharply outlines their pivotal position in the markets — moving Funds from supplying banks to using banks. Several accommodators actually make markets, since they are willing to trade Funds either way at quoted rates where close correspondent relations exist, regardless of their own

---

[1]The figures in this section covering the early 1960's are based on the study by Dorothy M. Nichols covering the period September, 1959 – September, 1963, cited on page 16. The figures for the last half of the 1960's are based on the "46 Bank Series" published in the *Federal Reserve Bulletin*. These data are supplemented by the call reports and other data collected by the System. Some estimates have also been made.

money position. Average daily two-way trading in Funds purchased and resold by individual banks on the same day ranged between $200 and $500 million at these banks in the early 1960's, and on balance, they absorbed $300 million net in their own positions. Two-way trading by accommodators located in other Federal Reserve districts ranged between $80 and $240 million on a daily average basis, but these banks generally balanced out in position. They were usually nonborrowers and accommodated by supplying Funds during periods of tightness and absorbing Funds during periods of ease. Two-way trading by both groups of accommodating banks approximated 25 to 30 percent of all Funds activity in the first half of the 1960's.

Substantial increases in the volume of Funds traded by accommodating banks have occurred during recent years. By the close of the 1960's, two-way trading at the several largest banks cited above had more than doubled, ranging between $800 million and $1.5 billion on the average. Fivefold increases in volume were reported at the banks outside New York. Two-way trading on an average day reached a level of $1 to $1.7 billion. The increase reflects not only more trading by the banks but an increase in the numbers doing an accommodating business. There was also a marked increase in the number of outside banks making net purchases. This volume averaged between $2 and $3 billion with five Chicago banks accounting for one-third to one-half of the increase.

Most of the Funds trading continues to be concentrated in a relatively small number of banks. About 45 large banks, a third of which have deposits of $1 billion or over, account for close to two-thirds of all transactions. It is these banks that have the greatest impact on the money market. (Some lessening of concentration has been noted in the last few years as regional trading has been developed by more correspondent systems.) Although the average dollar volume of the transactions of most of the other banks, in aggregate, is relatively small and does not have a substantial impact on the general money market, their operations play a continuous role that is at least marginally important to the reserve management of most of the 350-odd regular participants. These large banks each accomplish daily average purchases and sales of $10 million or over, depending upon the tightness or ease of the market, while the large majority of participants each purchase or sell an average of less than $2 million a day.

The importance of the New York banks as intermediaries is reflected in the fact that about 40 percent of the transactions of all out-of-town banks are with banks in the city. The volume of trading among New York City banks is relatively small — usually less than 20 percent of their total transactions. Interbank purchases of Funds within New York City normally average about $150 million a day and are roughly comparable to the amount purchased by them from nonbanks in the city. Transactions with banks outside the city comprise the largest share of New York City activity—about 75 to 80 percent of both purchases and sales. New York banks in the early 1960's sold only small amounts of Funds to nonbanks, but this practice showed a marked increase during the past several years. Outside banks, on the other hand, have at times been substantial sellers to nonbanks, and the volume of such transactions rises to peaks at times of heavy dealer financing needs.

In the districts outside New York City,[1] Funds traded locally within the same Federal Reserve district range on the average between 20 and 30 percent of total activity. The San Francisco and Chicago districts, however, as noted earlier, may report somewhat larger percentages of local trades, and in several districts — Atlanta, Kansas City, and Minneapolis — trades within the district usually represent only a modest percentage of the total. Many of the banks outside New York still tend to rely fairly heavily on New York banks both as a source for and disposal of Funds. Nevertheless, in some cases, there is a fair proportion of trading across district lines to points other than New York City.[2] The reliance on New York has tended to diminish during the last two years to the extent that accommodators outside the city have balanced more purchases and sales in their trading areas. Smaller correspondents who deal with accommodators report some cost savings in transactions, as compared with previous arrangements.

Interdistrict trading patterns emerging with the development of the Funds market reflect the usual contrasts. The New York,

[1] For details of trading in the various districts, see Bibliography.

[2] One large holding company in the Minneapolis district arranges purchases and sales for its members through the Bank of America with appropriate entries to reserve accounts at the Federal Reserve Bank of Minneapolis. A substantial number of the trading banks in the district are members of the holding company.

Chicago, and San Francisco districts absorb and supply the largest amount of Funds. For long periods of time, New York and Chicago have been net borrowers and San Francisco a net supplier. The New York City banks have purchased net as much as $1.6 billion on an average day in recent years.

The Chicago and San Francisco districts generally do not report a net position (+ or -) of more than $600 million. Most of the other districts report either a net inflow or outflow that averages up to $150 million a day in most statement weeks. Whether these districts are users or suppliers depends largely upon seasonal forces and payment flows throughout the year. At times, however, it may reflect changing policies of large banks in particular districts. During the last two years, heavy net purchases of the largest banks in the Minneapolis district have changed the district from a net seller to a net buyer.

The net Funds position of a district depends to some extent on a district's banking structure since large banks tend to be net buyers and small banks net sellers, or exclusively sellers. In the New York and San Francisco districts, a relatively large percentage of total deposits is held by very large banks while in Kansas City and Atlanta, the larger banks account for a relatively small proportion of total deposits. The size and continuity of the market depend to a considerable extent on the relatively large number of small banks that sell funds to a relatively small number of large banks.[1]

FEDERAL FUNDS VS. BORROWING AT RESERVE BANKS

On an average day in the late 1920's, Federal Funds traded for all member banks ranged from about 4 to 10 percent of required reserves. During the 1960's this ratio averaged about 12 percent in the early years and 27 percent toward the end of the decade. By this measure, trading in Funds has become of substantially greater relative importance than in earlier periods. At the same time the reserve requirement level is about 20 percent higher than in the 1920's.

[1]J. A. Cacy, "Tenth District Banks in the Federal Funds Market," *Monthly Review,* Federal Reserve Bank of Kansas City, November, 1969, pp. 10-20.

If the daily average volume of discounts and of trading in Federal Funds are combined, the total in the 1920's reached at times about 50 percent of required reserves in contrast to about 12 percent on heavy trading days in the 1950's, and 35 percent in the late 1960's. This indicates that borrowings from the Reserve banks made up a substantially larger part of the reserve base in the credit superstructure of the 1920's.

It should also be noted that borrowings from the Reserve banks during periods of expansion in the 1950's and 1960's averaged about $100 million less than in the late 1920's. However, the composition of total borrowing as suggested by the figures above was reversed; the ratio of Federal Funds to borrowings in the 1920's was about one to four; and now it is eight to ten to one. It may be said that in the 1920's Federal Funds were considered a supplement to discounting, but that in the 1960's discounting had become a supplement to trading in Federal Funds. Although transactions in Federal Funds relieve the individual bank from use of the discount window, they do not relieve the banking system as a whole from reliance on the Federal Reserve.

MARKET GROWTH REFLECTED IN "BORROWING FROM OTHERS"

The Weekly Condition Report of Large Commercial Banks[1] on Wednesday dates shows their borrowings from Federal Reserve banks and their borrowings from others separately from 1953 to July, 1969 (See Chart VII), when the series was revised.[2] "Borrowings from Others" during this period included largely commercial bank sources in most districts. In some, however, it reflected varying amounts borrowed from nonbanks.

A comparison of these borrowings with Funds purchases reported by weekly reporting banks suggests that Funds purchases

---

[1]This series included only member banks until 1966. After that date, nonmember commercial banks of comparable size are included.

[2]The weekly reporting banks now report a new liability item "Federal Funds Purchased." This caption also includes securities sold under repurchase agreement. No breakdown is supplied. The new caption when combined with "Borrowings from Others" is not comparable with the old series. Some components are reported on a different basis. See *Federal Reserve Bulletin*, August, 1969, pp. 642-46.

on Wednesdays from 1953 until 1966 ranged from 50 to 100 percent of the total borrowed from sources other than the Federal Reserve.[1] The identity of Funds purchases and borrowings from others was consistently reasonably close in all Federal Reserve districts except New York and Chicago, and transactions were largely interbank. The substantial differences between Funds purchases and "Borrowings from Others," reported with frequency by the New York City banks and in more limited amounts on occasion by banks in some other districts, reflect borrowings from corporations and other nonbank sources.[2] This borrowing generally took the form of a repurchase agreement with a maturity of more than one day and was accomplished in Funds.[3]

After 1965, amounts reported under this caption, while reflecting substantial increases in interbank Funds transactions, comprised an increased variety of other types of borrowings from banks and nonbanks, the proceeds of which were available in Funds. The transactions were also more widely distributed among Federal Reserve districts and are another reflection of the growing acceptance of liability management. These borrowings included securities and loans sold under repurchase agreement, Euro-dollars borrowed, directly or through brokers, from banks abroad, and liabilities to banks' own branches in U.S. territories and possessions. Increased use was also made of the traditional correspondent bank loan. Estimates place the amount of the transactions close to $6 billion on many days during 1969. Interbank Funds transactions accounted for the balance of about $9 billion.

Since 1955, Funds purchases derived from the caption have represented an increasing proportion of the total amount of all member bank borrowing in all Federal Reserve districts. Between

---

[1] A comparison of loans to commercial banks plus loans to brokers and dealers on U.S. Government securities with Funds sales by the weekly reporting banks shows similar results for years for which comparable data are available within this period.

[2] Computed from Funds reports and weekly reporting member bank statements.

[3] These transactions were not reported in the regular Funds reports except on the first day. In the revised weekly reporting series, continuing contracts are reported on each reporting date.

1953 and 1958, the amount borrowed in the form of Funds[1] on Wednesday dates doubled, almost tripled from 1963 to 1968, doubling again by mid-1969. The rise may be overstated because prior to the Comptroller's ruling in 1956, which classified Funds purchases as borrowings, many banks classified as investments those Funds transactions accomplished with underlying collateral.

CHART VII

TREASURY BILL HOLDINGS AND BORROWING 1953-1969
WEEKLY REPORTING MEMBER BANKS

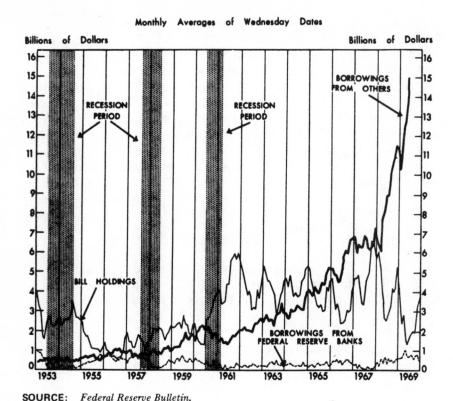

Monthly Averages of Wednesday Dates

SOURCE: *Federal Reserve Bulletin.*

[1] Partly estimated for some of the years shown.

Also, double counting may be a factor. Meanwhile, although borrowing from the Reserve banks rose in response to credit restraint during the cyclical upturns, it did not reach levels attained in the first half of 1953 until 1969. This development underscores greater continuing reliance by an increasing number of member banks on Funds transactions in preference to borrowing at the Reserve banks, and/or reliance on various other forms of borrowings, particularly during periods of credit restraint. It also shows the marked decline in relative importance of the use of Treasury bills after 1965 in adjusting reserve positions.

FACTORS INFLUENCING VOLUME OF FUNDS TRADING

The chief factor influencing the postwar growth of the Funds market has been the alteration of the institutional framework of the money market and the related changes in institutional practice generally described earlier.

In addition, certain technical modifications affecting bank operating practice, like those relating to the computation of required reserves and the net reductions in the level of required reserves, should be cited. These actions have made possible a larger volume of Funds transactions by the banking system as a whole without resorting to a larger volume of borrowing at the Reserve banks than occurred during the immediate postwar period.

Other technical factors affecting the market include the excess profits tax, arbitrage, and changes in check collection schedules. The two latter factors have been responsible for fluctuations in the volume of trading at various times.

A number of general factors have also been important in the market's growth. These include Federal Reserve policy, trends and fluctuations in interest rates, interbank competition, Treasury operations, variations in the level of float, and improvement in the System's and the commercial banks' wire transfer facilities. It is not possible, however, to assess the relative importance of either technical or general factors in furthering growth or development of breadth in the market.

Computation of Reserves

Beginning in March, 1942, banks located in central Reserve or Reserve cities were allowed to average reserves for weekly periods rather than semiweekly, a regulation in effect since the end of 1927.

In July, 1942, the Board amended Regulation D, relating to member banks' reserves, under the authority of an Act of Congress which became effective July 7.[1] The Federal Reserve Act (see Appendix A) permitted reserves of member banks to be checked against and withdrawn to meet existing liabilities. Observers believed that this provision was nullified to some extent by a proviso in Paragraph 9 of Section 19, which prohibited making new loans or paying dividends while reserves were deficient. A number of banks were hesitant about utilizing any portion of their required reserves even for a day unless they refrained from making new loans. This policy arose from bank directors' fear of personal liability for possible loss on loans. Many banks, because of the wide daily fluctuations in reserves, followed a practice of maintaining at all times a large volume of excess reserves. The amended law by eliminating the proviso permitted banks more flexibility in managing their reserves and loans and investments.

In October, 1949, all Reserve System member banks were permitted to offset a deficiency in one reserve computation period with excess in the next reserve period, provided that the deficiency carry-over did not exceed 2 percent of the required reserves of the first period. The provision for a longer period for averaging reserves and the privilege of carrying deficiencies from one period to the next facilitate the management of the reserve balances of member banks and the fuller use of the banks' available funds.

While these technical changes affecting reserve use or reserve computation made it easier for banks to make their own adjustments without borrowing in the Funds market or at the discount window, they also provided — along with other methods of adjusting bank reserves — a broader base for accomplishing Funds transactions, or using Funds during periods of continuing credit demands. To this extent these changes have been a factor in providing favorable

[1]Public Law 656 (Section 3) 77th Cong., 2d Sess., Chapter 488.

conditions for greater breadth of the Funds market in the 1950's. The change to a biweekly instead of a semimonthly reserve computation period for country banks in 1959, which led to a "double settlement" every other Wednesday, had little measurable effect on total activity.

Reductions in Levels of Required Reserves

Since the Accord, net reductions in reserves required against demand and time deposits and the inclusion of vault cash in the computation of reserves allowed since 1960 have jointly released a substantial volume of reserves for investment. The reductions in required reserves, usually complementing open market operations, have been made to initiate or develop more fully a policy of ease, provide for growth needs, diminish inequities in position of city and country banks, and, on occasion, to meet seasonal needs. The results in both level and structure of reserve requirements have provided a more flexible framework for credit expansion, in contrast to those of the historically high levels of the 1930's and early postwar periods, which had been designed to absorb the excess reserves associated with the Depression and World War II.

Against the basically strong aggregate demand for bank credit, which has generally been characteristic of the period following the reduction in reserves, the actions have had more than a transitory effect upon the volumes of Funds activity. They have contributed to increasing the dimensions of the Funds market.

The immediate result of a reduction in required reserves is to increase the effective supply of Funds available for trading. Given a continued broad demand for bank credit, the money market banks rapidly use the reserves released to repay Reserve bank borrowings and to consolidate and expand their operating positions. The less aggressive banks, on the other hand, retain their excess reserves for a somewhat longer period and expand their loans and investments only gradually. While money market banks soon become net buyers of Funds once more, the smaller banks are in a better position to meet these demands. As a result, Funds trading increases.

In recent years, one reflection of this enlarged activity is that Funds have become a significant feature of the secondary reserves of many banks. The growth in sales has been greater than the decline in excess reserves. The decline in excess reserves since 1951, as outlined in Chart VIII, has paralleled the expansion and changing structure of the Funds market.

The movement toward lower levels of excess reserves has been generally steady.[1] Although other factors have also influenced the administration of excess reserves, the Funds market has enabled the banks to make more rapid adjustments in their money positions. With the access that the market provides for the disposal and use of discretionary reserves, banks have become more confident in holding smaller amounts. The tendency to utilize reserves more fully in each

CHART VIII
EXCESS RESERVES AS A PERCENT OF REQUIRED RESERVES
(Averages of Daily Figures)
All Member Banks, U.S.

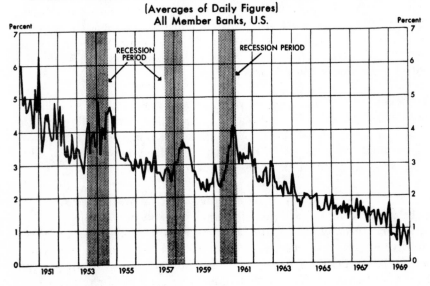

SOURCE: Federal Reserve Bulletin

[1]The ratio of demand balances due from banks to total deposits also declined, suggesting that the decline in excess reserves is real and not simply a transfer of funds from one nonearning asset to another. The decline in the correspondent balances, however, is not as large as the volume of Funds sold.

succeeding cycle has contributed to increasing supplies of Funds even during periods of restraint. In part, this is a reflection of the increase in the average size of member banks and of the increasing participation in straight Funds transactions or repurchases with dealers by smaller country banks which have characteristically held most of the excess reserves.

Participation now includes significant percentages of banks with deposits between $10 and $50 million. In some districts, a high percentage of banks with less than $10 million in deposits currently trade Funds. The typical movement of Funds runs from the smaller country banks and smaller city banks to the large banks in the Nation's financial centers. Some of these smaller banks, however, have now become more fully invested, expecting to support their positions by securing Funds from accommodating banks. In 1951, average deposit size of member banks had increased more than fivefold, reaching $58 million, and 454 banks held deposits of $100 million or more. As size increases, management of money position tends to become sharper. Banks in this size group account for close to 90 percent of the volume of both gross and net Funds purchases.

Profits in Rate Differentials

As the market developed in the postwar period, it has at times offered short-term profit opportunities to participants, stimulating Funds transactions as some banks take long or short positions in contemplation of rate movements. When there is considerable daily fluctuation in rate patterns, some of the larger Reserve city banks and country banks conduct transactions to capture rate profits. Funds are purchased when the rate softens in anticipation of selling them in the next day or two at firmer rates. Alternatively, banks have permitted limited cumulative deficits to develop, covering the deficit when the rate softens. In some cases, cheaply acquired Funds are resold in the form of repurchase agreements with Government security dealers to maximize rate profits.

According to some market participants, a part of the expansion of the Funds market (particularly during the years from the close of the war to the Treasury-Federal Reserve Accord) was brought about by using Funds to play the pattern of rates established when the Government securities market was pegged. Some banks in recent periods have conducted similar operations when they anticipated a policy shift by the Reserve System or when new cash offerings of securities or market conditions provided appropriate opportunities, such as the "split discount rates" of 1955, 1956, and 1957.

Reserve settlement dates have also provided profit opportunities for aggressive country banks. Until 1959, country banks had midmonth and month end reserve settlement dates and the city banks settled each Wednesday. Only seldom did a midmonth or month end settlement date coincide with a Wednesday settlement date. Thus, opportunities were afforded country banks to acquire Funds at favorable rates when rate softening accompanied Reserve city settlements. Cheaply acquired Funds could be used to maintain an invested position, to cover a reserve deficit, or accumulate a surplus when country banks expected the Funds rate to firm during the ensuing reserve period for city banks.

From late 1959 to September 12, 1968, country banks settled on two-week periods which coincided every other Wednesday with the Reserve city banks, and rate softness appeared on the all-bank, or double settlement, Wednesdays. Opportunities to capture rate profits were thus diminished.

The steadier and firmer market on many single settlement Wednesdays for Reserve city banks during this period resulted in large part from country banks buying Funds on these days. Similarly, actions of the country banks contributed to rate softness that appeared on double settlement dates, and at times, Funds were without a bid.

The Lag Accounting Reserve Plan

After considerable discussion, the so-called lagged method for computing required reserves was introduced with the statement week beginning September 12, 1968. Since that date, computation of reserve requirements has been based on:

1. Establishment of coincident one-week reserve computation periods for Reserve city banks and so-called "country banks";

2. Calculation of weekly average required reserves based upon average deposits two weeks earlier;

3. Calculation of weekly average reserves based upon average vault cash held two weeks earlier, along with the current week's balance at the Reserve banks; and

4. Provision for carrying forward to the next reserve week of either excesses or deficiencies averaging up to 2 percent of required reserves.

It was expected that these changes would reduce uncertainties, both for member banks and the Federal Reserve, about the amount of reserves required during the course of any reserve period. The automatic 2 percent carry-forward was expected to moderate pressures for reserve adjustments that developed, on occasion, near the close of a reserve period, causing sharp fluctuations in availability of day-to-day Funds and the Funds rate. Defensive open market operations would also be reduced.

Although the plan has helped reduce average excess reserves and has moderated the biweekly swings in reserves at country banks, the hopes have not been fully realized and some new problems have arisen. This was partly the result of caution on the part of many banks and partly because of unexpected money market developments as credit tightened in 1968 and 1969. Given the privilege of carrying over excesses as well as deficiencies, Reserve city banks with some frequency now operate with alternate deficit and surplus positions. In addition, these banks have tended to accumulate large amounts of excess reserves early in the statement week, thus tightening the Funds market. The market eases at the end of the same week as unutilized excess reserves are released. Such practices cause a rise of the Funds rate as the statement week opens and a fall near the end.(See Chart V.) When a number of the larger banks act together, these swings are exaggerated. Lagging required reserves two weeks behind deposits has also affected the course of intramonth deposit flows. This pattern usually ranges from a high at the beginning of the month to a low in the middle and rises again at month's end. Pressure on reserves is thus intensified at midmonth, and excessive ease arises at the close of the month unless offset by System operations. The lag plan to date has consequently placed greater demands on the Funds market as well as tending to increase the need for defensive open market operations within most statement weeks and at other times during a month.

It is quite possible that in the future each week's unutilized deficit and surplus carryovers may tend to become more equal, reducing the amplitude in the excess reserve swings and, consequently, reducing fluctuations in the Funds rate.[1]

Related to change in reserve computation are the recommendations of the lengthy and exhaustive study by the Committee for the Reappraisal of the Discount Mechanism, some of which liberalized the use of the discount window. An appreciably larger volume of Federal Reserve credit supplied through discounting may reduce the demand for Funds except in periods of restraint. During periods of neutrality and ease the Funds rate may fall below the discount rate with the same frequency as it did prior to 1964. More banks may make their reserve adjustments at the Federal Reserve bank than in the Funds market.

Final conclusions about the implications for changes in the Funds market resulting from new procedures in calculating reserves must await more experience. Similarly, conclusions about the market implications of possible changes in the discount mechanism including rate policy must await final decisions as well as experience.

Trends and Fluctuations in Interest Rates

Since the close of World War II, interest rates have fluctuated over a wide range, and the absolute levels have moved higher. The

---

[1]Some observers, however, believe that the adoption of coincident one-week reserve periods for all banks may simply make more frequent the exaggerated swings in the Funds market that in the past have been common on the old double settlement dates. See "The New Settlement Arrangements for Member Banks," *The Morgan Guaranty Survey*, May, 1968, pp. 3-5.

increases have been reflected in yields of all classes of money market instruments. In the late 1960's, rates either reached peaks which had not been achieved since 1921 or set new record highs. The bulk of the movement occurred in the last half of the 1960's.

TABLE IV

YIELDS ON SHORT-TERM MONEY MARKET INVESTMENTS

Type of Investment (3-Month Maturities except Federal Funds)	Yields Percent Averages of Daily Offering Rates	
	1961	1969
Treasury Bills	2.36	6.64
Commercial Paper	2.97	7.83
Finance Paper	2.68	7.16
Bankers' Acceptances	2.81	7.61
Certificates of Deposit* (Secondary Market)	3.07	8.05
Federal Funds (Effective Rate)	1.96	8.22

*C.D. yields are for April-December, 1962, when the series was initiated, and 1969 data are averages of representative weekly offering rates based on the Salomon Brothers' & Hutzler series. All other data: *Federal Reserve Bulletin.*

To the extent that they have been influenced by changes in interest rates, Funds transactions have been affected more by the erratic behavior of the Treasury bill rates (arising in some years partly because of significant increases in nonbank demand) than by changes in their levels. Thus, more country banks have shifted to the Funds market from Treasury bills to avoid the cost of selling and subsequently repurchasing, the risk of exposure to market loss, and the inconvenience when adjusting reserve positions within the settlement period (two weeks until September 12, 1968). Repurchase agreements with nonbank dealers have also been used to an increasing extent by many banks outside New York. Rates on these transactions are usually more profitable for the seller than straight Funds sales. Changes in levels of rates, however, seem to be of some importance in inducing smaller banks to enter or withdraw from the Funds market. On the other hand, the spread between Treasury bill yields and the Funds rate is frequently a significant factor in attracting investment to one or the other instrument. In part, the demand for Funds by many banks had arisen from the pressure on their deposits as corporation treasurers and local government units drew down their balances and invested them in Treasury bills or arranged repurchases with dealers or even sold their balances "as Funds" as interest rates rose. There has been a growing diversity in both the number and the type of investor participating in the money market.

CHART IX
SELECTED SHORT TERM MONEY MARKET RATES

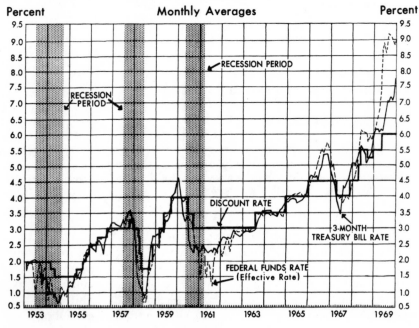

SOURCE: Federal Reserve Bank of New York.

Investment in open market commercial paper and acceptances by the banks as alternatives has been relatively less popular (despite the recent increases in outstandings and market activity) because of the changed character of those markets compared with previous periods, as noted earlier. These developments also underscore the shifting toward Funds as an investment medium in preference to Treasury bills or other money market instruments when surplus funds become available.

Excess Profits Tax, 1951-1953

In 1951, the Bureau of Internal Revenue ruled that Funds purchases, like other forms of borrowing, could be included by the buying banks in their "capital base" when calculating their excess profits tax liabilities. There is no concrete evidence that banks increased their volume of Funds transactions relative to other forms of borrowing, or entered the market for the first time for the express purpose of reducing their tax liability or avoiding payment of the tax. Trading in Funds, however, provided an easy method and, at times, was used in conjunction with other steps as a profitable method of avoiding the tax. Perhaps a few large banks bid aggressively for Funds during this period and supplemented their borrowing at the Reserve banks to establish a larger "capital base." However, the inclusion of Funds purchases in the "capital base" was largely a collateral benefit, and the basic forces stimulating expansion of the market lie elsewhere.

Inasmuch as the amount of excess reserves is relatively small, the purchase and sale of Funds do not relieve the banking system, however much they may relieve the individual bank, of borrowing from Reserve banks, particularly during periods of credit restraint. One reflection of System policy, which was in a restrictive phase during much of the excess profits tax period, was an increased amount of borrowing from the Reserve banks. This was also a period of bank and business expansion. Available data do not indicate that Funds purchases grew more rapidly in volume than borrowing from the Reserve banks or correspondents during the excess profits tax period.

Interbank Competition

Strong competition among the money banks to improve their relative position or to maintain their size and prestige in the postwar period has furthered the expansion of the Funds market. Also, this competition has contributed to the change in the structure of the market. An increasing number of these banks have developed outright a limited trading position in Funds to enable them to provide services (including supplying or buying Funds) to their correspondent banks or business customers. More recently, some of these banks have aggressively sold their Funds service, viewing it as a "new business service" and, in some cases, a feature of operations where volume alone is a matter of pride. Mergers and consolidations among some of the money market banks have sharpened the competition by aiding the development of larger Funds positions.

Gross purchases by the accommodating banks as a group during the last two years averaged between $5 and $8 billion daily in many statement weeks, an amount which substantially exceeds the activity of this group in the early 1950's. As the banking system of the early postwar period changed from investor to lender, the need for liquidity increased. More banks came to rely on the Funds market to supply this need. These banks, along with others, use part of the resources of other banks (in the form of Funds) in servicing certain customers to a greater or lesser degree at various times. Disparities in the relative size of individual banks were greater in the 1950's than during the 1920's and became even more pronounced in the early 1960's. The shifting temporary strains which develop under such conditions and which tend to be offset by Funds transactions are a natural consequence of unit banking.

Debt Management and Treasury Operations

The observation is frequently made that the U.S. Treasury is the largest and most active single borrower in financial markets. As such, debt management decisions, no matter how carefully made and how well executed, cannot avoid creation of market uncertainty and some "churning" during the adjustment and absorption period of Treasury operations at particular times. Treasury bill rates tend to be quite sensitive to the reflex effect.

At various times throughout the postwar years, the bill rate has behaved with some degree of arbitrariness, reflecting the varying strength of nonbank demand, the reinvestment demand for bills at times of large refundings and the substantial variation in supplies of bills — more recently the use of strip bills — and the introduction of new bill cycles. Since its introduction in 1961, the negotiable certificate of deposit, along with the increased variety of shorter term Federal agency paper, has been added to the group of money market instruments which compete with Treasury bills for cash balances of nonbank and other investors and has resulted in some variable upward pressure on short-term rates. In contrast, the rate on Funds during these periods has exhibited greater stability and has frequently been relatively more attractive, encouraging the use of Funds as an outlet. The expanded volume of debt operations, as well as a larger volume of trading, has increased the demand for Funds. Part of the growth in total Funds activity stems from these influences.

Improved administration of Treasury balances at commercial banks and Reserve banks has generally provided a better distribution of balances in depositaries and has relieved the intensity of pressures which formerly was concentrated in a relatively small group of banks. The introduction of the "C" depositories in 1955 made a marked improvement. Increased flows of Government funds over the last ten years, arising from debt operations and from regular disbursements and receipts, however, have subjected a fairly broad group of banks to moderate pressures or provided them with excess reserves. Thus, Treasury operations may be considered another factor which contributed to participation in the Funds market. During certain years, the frequency and amplitude of the swings in Treasury deposits have been a special factor in increasing the volume of Funds traded.

System Operating Policy

Another factor that has had some influence on the development and growth of the Funds market has resulted from the centralization of open market operations of the System Account in New York, along with the growing use and volume of open market operations in Government securities as the dominant policy instrument. Centralization of open market operations in New York has been in process since 1922, when the Federal Open Market Committee emerged as an informal arrangement. The Banking Act of 1935 merely gave final legal status to its development. This, along with the gravitational pull of the financial and business center, which had been developing in New York since the mid-1800's, gave further impetus to the location and expansion of Government securities and acceptance dealers in New York. Thus, all facilities existing outside New York for trading Governments have come to be based on the New York market in respect both to quotations and breadth. Except for the relatively small amount of orders that is matched off by bank and investment firms in local or regional markets, trading is done ultimately with or through offices or branches of Government securities dealers and dealer banks in New York City, Chicago, and one in Los Angeles.

As a result, a wider group of investors has been encouraged to use Funds for settlement of transactions. These Funds have, in many instances, come from an interdistrict source. The unwillingness or the inability of the New York banks to meet all of the dealers' financing needs forced them to develop a network of Funds supplies outside New York City.

Reduction in Federal Reserve Deferred Availability Schedule

The Federal Reserve check collection time schedule was reduced from a maximum of up to eight days to a maximum of three days in 1939, and to two days in 1951. These reductions have been an important factor in the rise of the average level of float from one of $500 to $600 million in 1950, to one of $2 to $2.5 billion in the last five years. The amplitude of the swings in float has also increased, and monthly averages in recent years have moved between lows of $1.3 billion and highs of $3.4 billion. These short-run fluctuations have considerable impact at times on member bank reserves. Frequently float is unevenly distributed, so that there is little relationship between the float change at a particular bank and the national pattern. Thus, no bank can regularly expect with any certainty any sharing in total float swings. Even those who attempt to estimate the change may experience unexpected reserves or a need for reserves and must resort to the Funds market and other adjustment methods to balance out positions. The general importance of Funds in this connection is substantiated by patterns of

Funds traded, which tend to show with some frequency a marked intramonthly rise and fall in positive association with float peaks and troughs. Thus, from one point of view, Funds transactions can be considered a refinement of the clearing process.

In periods of the year when the average monthly float shows wide changes that result in a general surplus or shortage of reserves among the smaller banks, they have historically used surplus funds to retire borrowings at the Reserve banks or to increase correspondent balances in money centers. During the last several years, however, a number of these banks have sharpened their practices and have utilized Funds sales to dispose of excess reserves. Thus, the flow of banking balances, which moved to New York in some volume at midmonth during certain periods of the year, has shown a tendency to diminish. Much less frequently these banks will borrow Funds in relatively small amounts, usually preferring to use the discount window to cover deficits.

Regularly recurring fluctuations in float seem to be well integrated in money market operations, and the impact of such fluctuations is cushioned by transactions in the Funds market. Federal Reserve offsets are made when feasible. Serious distortions can and do occur, however, from unexpected fluctuations in float. Through the nature of the float process, most of the unanticipated fluctuations produce larger magnitudes than expected. This is usually caused by weather variations and delivery delays resulting from strikes or other causes. More frequently than not, an unexpectedly large increase will be followed by an unusually large decrease. The sale of Funds or the purchase of Treasury bills, if the surplus of reserves persists, accounts for some of the sharp drops in rates and the appearance of market ease that occurs at times. As float disappears, a sharp tightening of the market occurs, resulting in an atmosphere of greater firmness than had originally prevailed as banks readjust their positions.

Improvement of Wire Transfer Facilities

Since the close of the war, the Federal Reserve's wire transfer facilities have been steadily improved. The transmission time over the wire was reduced and the volume of messages which could be handled were increased. A high speed data transmission system

79

utilizing a computer switch began operation September 1, 1970. This system, currently several times faster than the old wire system, has virtually unlimited potentials for volume and speed.

The inauguration of the "bank wire" in 1950 by commercial banks has substantially improved communication between banks. The wire now links more than 250 banks in 69 principal cities. These developments have facilitated and encouraged the use of the Funds market, making possible rapid transfers to points of use and enlarging the framework of the money market.

Federal Reserve Policy

The 1950's and 1960's were periods of substantial year-to-year growth in the volume and scope of transactions in the Funds market. This growth, the attendant spread of knowledge about the market, the attractiveness of long periods of rising interest rates, and a large number of new entrants have tended to blur the cyclical pattern. With the unpegging of the Government securities market in March, 1951, System credit policy became more flexible and since that date has shifted between restraint and ease in response to developments in business.

Shifts in System credit policy influence the volume of Funds traded in the market. At the same time, these shifts influence other methods of reserve adjustment, and banks switch activities from one market to another in response to the interaction of changing rate relationships and the availability of reserves in terms of loan demand or investment opportunities. Available data fail to suggest that mere shifts from restraint to ease or the reverse have encouraged the use of Funds as an alternative to other methods of adjustment over the period as a whole. Aside from the years 1965, 1966, and 1969, Funds activity has been highest when the market is in a neutral position, neither very tight nor very easy. This reflects chiefly rate relationships which suggest no material profit advantage in alternative outlets.

The data showing the volume of transactions accomplished through the brokers (Table III), as well as data for a number of individual banks, indicate that the years of most rapid growth in the Funds market as its national emphasis developed were 1950 (80 percent higher than the previous year), 1951 (36 percent higher), and 1954 (18 percent higher). These were years when System policy for the most part reflected some phase of ease.

The year-to-year changes in the volume of Funds traded during periods of restrictive policy also show growth, but at a much diminished rate (except 1966 and 1969) compared with periods of ease. During 1952-1953, the volume of Funds traded through Garvin Bantel increased only 3 percent from one year to the next and in the substantially broader market of 1955-1957 about 10 percent. Activity decreased during the early phase of restraint in 1955 but remained substantially above the level of 1952-1953. Data available for a number of individual banks in New York City and Chicago, as well as for banks outside those areas, show the same general patterns.

Transactions data available since 1957 for a comprehensive sample of banks indicate that trading volume has increased about tenfold, and that the periods of ease — 1958, 1960-1965, and 1967 — produced record levels of Funds activity. The period of restraint in 1959 brought about a drop in the average level of trading compared with ease in 1958, but the level, like that in 1955, remained substantially above that in any preceding period.

The severely restrictive credit policy in 1966 and 1969 are exceptions and produced new record levels of transactions, large additions to the numbers of banks using the market, and steady premium bids for Funds. The brokers' data also follow this pattern, but the increases are larger, reflecting in part more double counting — a characteristic of both bank and broker figures as two-way trading expanded in recent years.

For several reasons, it is difficult to see a direct functional relationship between Funds trading and credit policy in both the 1950's and the 1960's. Although there have been periods of ease since the Accord about which generalizations can be made, it is not possible to distinguish accurately the increase that came about primarily because of a growing awareness of the Funds market on the part of country banks from the increase due to expanded trading in Funds by all banks.

Also, the influence of the widened demand for Funds by nonbanks and corporate participants cannot be isolated satisfactorily. In other words, the structure of the market changed somewhat from one period to another (including both ease and restraint) as did the practices and policies of institutions participating in the market. Considering these qualifications, however, the impression remains and data suggest that Funds trading developed at a faster rate during the periods of ease than it did during periods of restraint. Both the trough and peak of the cycles which may be accompanied by extremely easy or quite tight markets, respectively, are excepted. This behavior of the market can most readily be explained in a review of the principal supply and demand factors and the structural changes which characterized the market during these periods.

a. MONETARY RESTRICTION: 1952-1953, 1955-1957, and 1958-1960.[1] Money market reaction to restrictive credit policies was generally the same in each of these periods. Open market operations, as is customary, were used to work down the supply of excess reserves, and reserves to meet the increased demand for loans and investments became less readily available and more costly. Reserves continued to be available at a price as restrictive policy in the postwar period has generally been designed to limit credit growth, not to bring about a net reduction.

Greater use was made of borrowings at the Reserve banks, and borrowing tended to involve a large but shifting number of banks. Borrowings outstanding, on the average, ranged from moderate to substantial amounts, and there was frequently no rate advantage in using Funds in preference to the discount window.

Banks tended to conserve their reserves and employed them more continuously to serve their lending areas. They tended to be reluctant Funds sellers, afraid that they could not buy Funds if needed. The banks also operated within their rules and dealt only with those with whom they had established lines. However, some increase in the supply occurred as more banks used the market as an outlet for excess reserves.

---

[1]March, 1952 — June, 1953; January, 1955 — November, 1957; August, 1958 — January, 1960. See *Annual Report* of Board of Governors of the Federal Reserve System for each of these years for a description of these periods.

In contrast to periods of ease, the demand for Funds tended to intensify, while the supply became smaller and less fluid. An increase in the volume of Funds traded occurred, but at a slower rate, since expansion in the volume of Funds traded during these periods was dependent indirectly upon borrowings at the Reserve banks and since for considerable periods Funds were no cheaper than borrowings at the discount window.

During restrictive periods, the demand for Funds has resulted from a substantial increase in the demand for loans and investments by a greater variety of users and from some need by aggressive banks to operate on a borrowed reserve base to sustain expansion or to hold their competitive positions. Seasonal pressures in a period of rising business activity also place added strain on the adjustment of bank reserves at particular times.

As credit policy becomes more restrictive, alternative money market outlets may become more attractive than Funds. Toward the close of restrictive periods until those in 1966 and 1969, rates of other money market instruments frequently exceeded the Funds rate and absorbed some reserves that otherwise would have been sold in the market.

b. MONETARY RESTRICTION: 1965-1966 and 1968-1969.[1] These restraint periods are distinguished from their predecessors in several respects, all of which influence activity in the market. First, credit policy was pursued with more severity for a longer period than previously. This is particularly true of the latter period. Second, the discount rate was used sparingly and was below other market rates most of the time. Third, Regulation Q was used in addition to other policy instruments to prevent acquisition or force

---

[1]December, 1965 — November, 1966; January, 1968 — December, 1969. See *Annual Report* of the Board of Governors of the Federal Reserve System for these years for a description of these periods.

In late June, 1968, the Federal Open Market Committee directed that open market operations be conducted with a view to accommodating tendencies for short-term interest rates to decline and for somewhat less firm money market conditions to develop in connection with enactment of fiscal restraint legislation and to facilitate adjustment to reduction of Federal Reserve bank discount rates (in mid-August) with provision for modification depending on the course of bank credit developments. From then until mid-December, the account supported prevailing money market conditions.

runoffs in CD's. Fourth, the banks were more innovative in devising methods of cushioning the impact of policy. Federal Funds transactions, Euro-dollar borrowing, commercial paper sales, and loan repurchase agreements experienced major growth in the banks' search for reserves. Finally, since fiscal policy in 1966 continued to be stimulative on balance and was at best neutral in 1969, a greater burden was placed on monetary policy in restraining economic activity.

Trading, contrary to patterns during restraint in the past, accelerated, and the volume of Funds transactions reached new high levels in each period. There was aggressive bidding for Funds at progressively higher rates. The intense pressure for credit and the changing relationship among short-run investment or borrowing alternatives forced a further rapid, although evolutionary, expansion of the market.

Exceptionally heavy corporate and state and local borrowing in capital markets and a particularly sharp increase in business loans at commercial banks characterized both periods. Associated with the demand for credit, short- and long-term rates rose sharply and almost continuously. The advance in rates was more rapid as monetary restraint intensified and reinforced the upward pressures arising from heavy credit demands. Curbing inflationary expectations was a problem in both periods, but their perseverance in 1969 was unusually stubborn.

To slow bank credit expansion, open market operations were used to contract bank reserves. Regulation Q ceilings which were below market rates on competitive instruments at the beginning of 1969 were not changed. Pressure on CD runoffs increased as market rates rose with the intensification of the restrictive policy. In this instance, the Regulation was used directly to restrain credit expansion in contrast to 1966 when it was used as a supplement to other policy instruments. Market rates then did not pierce the ceilings until near the end of the period. Prior to 1966 Regulation Q rates were generally accommodated to market rates.

The System also used selective measures. In July and September, 1966, it increased reserves on time deposits in excess of $5 million. Strong moral suasion was reflected in a letter dated

September 1, 1966, in which the System requested member banks to reduce business loan expansion instead of cutting further into holdings of securities. At the same time, it was noted that discount accommodation was available to support deposit shrinkage and prevent severe market stringency. Few banks took advantage of the offer. Most banks continued to show a strong preference for making adjustments with Federal Funds. In 1969, the System imposed reserves on Euro-dollars, narrowed bank use of repurchase agreements with nonbanks, announced proposals to make bank related commercial paper sales subject to Regulations D and Q, and narrowed the scope of Funds transactions.

Many interest rates, both short- and long-term, rose to the highest levels in this century. Sensitive rates, such as three-month Treasury bills, peaked at 8.12 percent, commercial paper at 9.25 percent, and bankers' acceptances at 9.00 percent in December, 1969. The effective rate on Funds was 9 to 9 ½ percent on many days during the last half of the year, and 3 to 3 ½ percentage points above the effective rate in 1966. At the bank counter, the rate on prime loans in June stood at 8 ½ percent, 2 percentage points above April, 1968. In the capital market, new long-term corporate Aaa bond yields reached 8.85 percent, and state and local bonds, 6.90 percent toward the end of the year. At the same time, outstanding 3-, 5-, and 10-year U.S. Treasury coupon securities sold to yield 8.51 percent, 8.33 percent, and 7.77 percent, respectively—the highest rates since the Civil War for these issues.

In this atmosphere the demand for Funds intensified, and the consistently high rate levels and yield advantage over Treasury bills induced many banks to sell larger amounts and encouraged additional banks to enter the market for the first time. There was also a significant increase in the number and variety of nonbanks in the market. Competition became very aggressive among city correspondents in developing Funds trading arrangements for their smaller correspondents. These arrangements increased the accessibility of the market to more banks, while higher rates and rising costs forced development of more efficient management of reserves, thus stimulating activity in the Funds market. The volume of interbank Funds transactions amounted to about $5 billion a day with some frequency in 1966 and probably $10 billion on many days in 1969. An increasing number of banks became net purchasers, especially in

1969. As noted earlier, Euro-dollar purchases and sales of bank related commercial paper to nonbanks reduced required reserves and increased velocity of deposits, thus helping support a larger volume of Funds trading.

The opportunity cost to the bank of meeting reserve needs—essentially the Funds rate and the amount of administrative pressure at the discount window—was higher in 1969 than in any other postwar year. The level of net borrowed reserves may be used as a rough index of these costs. In this measure the level of member bank borrowing from the Reserve banks generally reflects the degree of administrative pressure at the discount window. Net borrowed reserves stood at $872 million on a daily average basis. Daily borrowing from the Federal Reserve averaged $1,101 million, and excess reserves only $229 million. The average annual rate on Funds was 8.22 percent.

Prior to 1965, the Funds market operated largely as an alternative to Federal Reserve credit for borrowers and as an alternative to holding excess reserves or Treasury bills for lenders. During recent years, it has been used intensively for reserve adjustments to cover deficits in cash flows or to replenish excess reserves. In response to high and rising interest rates, more and more member and nonmember banks came to use the market as a secondary reserve investment, even substituting them not only for excess reserves but for short-term investment securities or in some cases lower levels of loans.

Rapid growth of the Funds market, which began after 1965, probably began to approach culmination in 1969. The high rates attracted more participants as sellers, thus increasing the dependability of the market as a source of borrowed money in a period of restraint. Flows through the market are now at record high levels; at least half of the member banks are participants along with the larger nonmembers. There remain many small banks which lack understanding of the market. As familiarity with the market develops, they may become participants. Funds volume, however, cannot be expected to grow as it has in recent years.

c. MONETARY EASE: 1953-1954 and 1957-1958.[1] During these periods of monetary ease, substantial amounts of reserves were made available to the banking system through open market operations and through reductions in required reserves. Borrowing at the Reserve banks was intermittent and limited to individual bank situations, with only a small amount outstanding on an average basis. In addition to the increase in volume, the supply of excess reserves was also more fluid. Some of the most sensitive interest rates — Funds and Treasury bills — were continuously below the discount rate.

Unlike earlier periods, in which recession policies of ease had merely diminished the disposition of banks to curtail credit, the banks in these periods were so liquid that they aggressively sought opportunities to employ idle balances at the Reserve banks. Under these conditions, many banks regularly offering Funds in the market relaxed their rules and dealt with banks with which they had no established lines, allowing the broker to arrange transactions on a "submit" or "show me" basis. In addition, throughout much of 1954 and in 1958, the Funds rate remained above the rate on three-month Treasury bills (as it frequently had during restrictive policy phases) and thus provided a further incentive on the supply side for trading in Funds. During periods of ease, a smooth flow of Funds at "good" rates — rates above minimum rates necessary to recover costs — tends to stimulate trading. Selling banks are willing to accommodate buyers because Funds are more readily available. Should the Funds be sold and subsequently be needed by the selling bank, they can usually be bought at the same or possibly a lower rate.

Sustained demands for Funds during the periods of ease have come from several sources. Borrowings by Government securities dealers tend to be larger when money market conditions are easier, reflecting the greater opportunities for profitable positions in securities when rates are falling than when rising. The larger borrowing by dealers in 1954, for example, supported a part of the demands for Funds by those banks particularly active in financing them. Nonbank dealer borrowings in 1954 and 1958 rarely fell below

---

[1]June, 1953 — January, 1955; November, 1957 — July, 1958. See *Annual Report* of the Board of Governors of Federal Reserve System for each of these years for a description of these periods.

$600 million and reached over $1.2 billion — two of the highest points up to that time in the postwar period. A large proportion of the borrowings was in Funds resulting from overnight or short-term "buy backs," arranged with banks outside New York. New York banks took substantial amounts of Funds into their operating positions, and this, to some extent, influenced their willingness to lend to dealers.

In addition, those banks that found themselves with temporary reserve deficiencies tended to turn to the Funds market rather than to the discount window because of the rate differential which existed during these periods of ease.

d. MONETARY EASE: 1960-1965.[1] In earlier periods of ease, credit policy was designed to a large extent with domestic considerations in mind. More recent periods, however, have required protection of the international position of the dollar in addition to encouragement of domestic recovery and expansion of economic activity. In previous recovery and expansionary periods, the System began to reduce monetary ease within four months of the business trough, but in the upturn — February, 1961, through November, 1965 — it was carried through 58 months of economic expansion. Although modified slightly in December, 1962, and to a greater degree in July, 1963, and November, 1964, when discount rates were raised and reserve availability lessened, monetary policy continued to be basically easy.

Monetary ease previously had been accompanied by low levels of the sensitive interest rates — Funds, Treasury bills, dealer loans, acceptances, commercial paper, and CD's. During most of the period, however, policy actions were designed to avoid downward pressures on the key short-term rates, which otherwise might have been forced to levels that would encourage short-term capital flows to foreign money centers, intensifying the balance of payments problem. After 1961, bill rates were pushed upward, on occasion, to diminish

---

[1]The shift toward monetary ease began in late February, 1960. Monetary ease was established by midsummer 1960. Ease was modified moderately in June, 1962, December, 1962, July, 1963, and November, 1964. See *Annual Report* of the Board of Governors of the Federal Reserve System for each of these years for a description of these periods.

spreads between rates in U.S. and foreign money centers, and fluctuations from week to week narrowed substantially. Open market operations in February, 1961, were broadened to include transactions in U.S. Government securities in the maturity range beyond one year. Reserve requirements were reduced at appropriate times to meet longer run growth needs and, at other times, to meet seasonal needs for reserves. Although long-term rates fluctuated in a narrow range, they declined moderately, on balance, from 1960 to 1964, despite the expansion of business. Downward pressure on these rates was influenced by the heavy flow of savings. Inflows of savings were encouraged by the increase in maximum rates permitted by Regulation Q on time and savings deposits and CD's. Both short- and long-term rates remained consistently above levels characteristic of previous periods of ease.

Money and financial flows have set new records since 1960. The relationship which developed between market rates and deposit interest rates from 1960 to 1965 influenced consumers to take a substantial share of increased holdings of financial assets in the form of time and savings deposits or share accounts. In earlier periods of expansion, increases in holdings of financial assets by individuals took the form of direct acquisitions of securities. In response to these developments, the composition of commercial bank assets changed rapidly, resulting in increased holdings of higher yield assets, such as mortgages and state and local government securities. Loan-deposit ratios moved higher, and banks on the whole developed more fully invested positions. Liquid asset ratios as conventionally defined fell. The increased individual bank need for liquidity under these conditions was met increasingly through the Funds market.

The volume of Funds activity rose sharply and reached new high levels of trading as the money market eased during the first half of 1960. As in earlier periods, the greater availability of reserves enabled the banks to purchase Funds to retire borrowings at the Reserve banks, and the demand for Funds for this and other purposes kept the rate at the ceiling for several months after yields on short-term Treasury bills had fallen somewhat below the discount rate. Trading tapered off moderately after mid-1960 but continued active, exhibiting larger short-run swings. Trading volume resumed its increase toward the close of 1961. Over the whole period 1960-1965, the volume of transactions tripled and all regions shared in the growth. The spread between the Funds rate and Treasury bill rate was generally favorable to Funds, and at the same time, the Funds rate frequently exhibited more stability than the bill rate, even though bill rate fluctuation narrowed substantially. The banks' need for liquidity was affected by new patterns of time and savings deposit liabilities and by growth in demand deposits.

Another factor which influenced the volume of trading in Funds was the policy adopted by some New York City banks in making substantial proportions of nonbank dealer loans available in the form of Funds. This policy was introduced about March, 1961, and became more liberal in 1962 as the banks became confident that an atmosphere of ease would continue. In 1965, all of the proceeds were generally made available in Funds. The change in policy was designed, in part, to expand dealer loan volume, which was more profitable under conditions of monetary ease, and also to meet increasing competition from lenders outside New York. Dealer positions were also heavier, and total borrowing needs expanded, reaching peaks of borrowing from New York City banks of over $1.5 billion on several dates. Dealer borrowings from corporations under repurchase agreements were also increased, and expansion in dealer transactions added further to the demand. New York City banks, under these conditions, were continuous demanders of Funds. Rates on Funds more clearly tended to move directly with the volume of net purchases by New York City banks — a factor holding the Funds rate above levels of earlier periods of ease.

Demand for Funds intensified in 1964 and 1965 in response to continued expansion in bank credit and other financial flows. In the fall of 1964, several aggressive banks willingly bid more than the discount rate on a number of occasions, establishing the premium bid as a feature of the market. Perhaps these banks preferred to make their adjustments in the Funds market rather than the discount window because they felt the Funds market afforded more privacy or because they had a shortage of convenient collateral. After March, 1965, it became increasingly common for banks to bid a premium for Funds. This and other sensitive short-term rates reached new high levels. The Funds rate almost continuously exceeded the Treasury bill rate by a significant margin, as it had (except in 1964) since the first half of 1962. The spread induced more banks to become sellers and increased trading. New entrants and a greater number of accommodators also stimulated large flows of Funds.

e. MONETARY EASE: 1966-1967.[1] An expansive policy was initiated again in late 1966 and was carried into the fourth quarter of 1967. Strong demand for bank loans resumed in the first quarter and remained relatively steady.

Throughout the period, banks rebuilt liquidity which they had drawn down sharply in 1966. Capital market calendars remained very heavy, and corporations also turned to the commercial paper market for larger amounts of Funds than previously. Athough both short-term and long-term rates receded from their peaks reached in the previous fall, long-term rates remained relatively high. Long-term rates resumed their rise in late winter, and during the spring they led short-term rates — for the first time in 20 years — back toward levels reached the previous year. The rise was spectacular. System policy depressed short-term rates for only a few months but failed to depress a continuous rise in long-term rates.

As credit ease was established, the Funds rate and the three-month Treasury bill rate dropped sharply and continued to decline until midyear 1967. Although the spread tended to narrow, the Funds rate remained above the Treasury bill rate. This reflected not only the demand to replenish liquidity positions but also the sizable contraction of market supplies of Treasury bills as taxes were paid and as the System Account bought securities in the open market to supply reserves. At midyear, the Funds rate leveled off at about 3.75 percent and Treasury bills at 3.50 percent.

During the second half of the year, the spread was reversed, and the bill rate exceeded the Funds rate. Reflecting Treasury needs, bill supplies were increased substantially while monetary policy remained easy. Banks used Funds to arbitrage Treasury bills, taking advantage of the large spread. Banks also continued to prefer to make their adjustments in the Funds market and at times paid a premium above the discount rate, although borrowing from the Reserve banks was generally cheaper.

---

[1]The shift toward ease began in November, 1966, and continued to early December, 1967. See the *Annual Report* of the Board of Governors of the Federal Reserve System, 1966 and 1967, for a description of this period.

As has been noted, the Funds rate remained continuously above the discount rate until April, 1967, and over the balance of the year, it exceeded the discount rate on a number of occasions. The stimulative policy was continued despite the high and rising levels of economic activity. As a carry-over from late fall 1966, the expansive policy in the first quarter was based on fear of a recession and was later justified as an aid to housing markets as well as an attempt to avoid intensifying problems in the British pound sterling.

High rate levels persisting throughout the year and ample credit availability, together with strong demands, provided an impetus to Funds transactions.

SUMMARY AND COMPARISONS OF FUNDS WITH MONEY MARKETS ABROAD

The Funds market has become a major part of the short-term money market in the United States. The origin was spontaneous, and development occurred in response to competitive forces in the private sector. Its organizational structure merely reflects the characteristics of this Nation's institutional environment. Thus, the market is a function of the unit banking system and a federation of the units by the Federal Reserve.

The Funds market satisfies the criteria of a money market. Supplies of temporarily idle cash that member banks seek to invest in earning assets are matched with the demand for such balances by banks and other financial insitutions who wish to adjust their liquidity position. The supply of Funds revolves, enabling the participants to rely on outside sources with confidence when adjusting positions and to avoid maintaining higher cash ratios than needed. Profit and price are the main considerations that direct flows through the market.

The Funds market contributes significantly to the integration of the unit banking system. It supplements reserve averaging, refines the clearing process, and makes the unit system more flexible and responsive to the broad range of domestic and foreign economic needs. Stated another way, the market gives the unit structure some of the advantages of branch banking. At the same time, it contributes to sharpening competition among the units.

Access to the Funds market makes banks more willing lenders in situations involving new investment. The unified nature of the market and its links with other divisions of the money market make possible more rapid transmission — to all parts of the financial community — of the interest rate responses and the changes in the availability of credit that flow from Federal Reserve policy actions. The Funds market may also be said to support more predictable behavior by the banks since use of the market tends to fall into patterns.

Short-term money markets abroad perform the same purposes as the Funds market but reflect different institutional structures. In the London market — the oldest — the clearing banks, which provide nearly all the bank credit, do not borrow from each other but compensate for fluctuations in their cash ratios by lending more or less to the discount houses. These, in turn, have access to the Bank of England. The cash reserves of the clearing banks are maintained at a customary 8 percent. About half of these reserves is "till money" and the other half is "bankers' deposits" — credits at the central bank. There is no margin of excess reserves in the system. Surpluses are absorbed by the Bank of England, and if additional funds are needed, it adds to its assets.

Professor Sayers, in commenting upon the London market,[1] has stated that if dealing in balances at the Bank of England were permissible, "and this is what the Federal Funds market comes to," the discount houses could be viewed as unnecessary. In further comment, Professor Sayers questions, "If a market of the Federal Funds type can take care of any redistribution of cash reserves required by the commercial banks, what is there left for a money market of the old type — a bill market — to do?" He states that a London dealer would point to two other functions now performed by him and his counterparts elsewhere. Sayers adds that the answer is also relevant to New York dealers, with proper qualification. The dealer would continue his earlier function in connection with acceptances but with reduced volume. With more accepting undertaken by the banks, his work is less significant. On the other hand,

---

[1]See R. S. Sayers *Central Banking after Bagehot,* Chapter 10, "The New York Money Market Through London Eyes," Oxford, 1957.

the function of making a market in "short-term government paper," which has grown during the last thirty years, is of much increased importance; and the dealers are valuable primarily because "they are buffers in the market for government paper." Their functions as intermediaries "dealing in bank cash is less vital though it does, incidentally, strengthen the markets for securities."

The Euro-dollar market, the newest short-term money market, provides the facilities for matching the demand for and the supply of dollar deposits in Europe. It is somewhat similar in concept to the Funds market and came into being without official initiative. The market is large — multibillion in size — and active. Several hundred banks — 50 percent of which are in Western Europe, Canada, and Japan — account for the bulk of the business. London is the focal point for transactions and the most prominent market center. In a sense, the market's growth is the result of controls imposed on currencies or credit systems by one or another government.

Euro-dollars are deposits of U.S. dollars in banks outside the United States, including overseas branches of American banks. Euro-dollars come into existence when an American or foreign owner of a deposit with a bank in the United States transfers funds to a foreign bank or a foreign branch of an American bank. The transaction transfers ownership of the deposit in the United States to a bank abroad and is offset by the institution's assumption of a liability payable in United States dollars. Total bank deposits in the United States remain unchanged, but an additional dollar deposit has been created abroad.

Additional Euro-dollars may be created if the foreign banking institution deposits the funds with another foreign bank — the original dollar deposit in the United States changing hands in the process. After making allowances for double counting, the Bank for International Settlements estimated a total of about $37.5 billion of such deposits denominated in dollars at year end 1969.

Normally, funds are placed in the Euro-dollar market because higher rates of interest can be earned there than on domestic time deposits or through other short-term investment outlets. Fully integrated and active foreign exchange markets permit banks to take in deposits denominated in foreign currencies, swap them into dollars, and then use the dollars in the Euro-dollar market. These transactions are hedged against adverse exchange fluctuations. This market, like the Funds market domestically, is of course only a part of the international market for short-term funds.[1]

During the last several years the market has increasingly been used as a source of borrowing short-term funds by large American banks to help meet domestic credit demands. Euro-dollars have also been used to adjust reserve positions as an alternative to purchasing Federal Funds particularly over weekends.

About 20 percent of Euro-dollar deposits in foreign branches of U.S. banks are currently overnight or call maturity. This percentage varies with the policy of individual banks and the availability of Euro-dollars. The percentage has been higher at times. The average maturity of such deposits is about two months. Borrowers anticipate the use of overnight or call money so that the proceeds are available in Funds on the day that they are needed.[2]

Even when Euro-dollars have been the highest-marginal-cost source of funds as they were consistently in 1969, many banks willingly paid the differential to help insure maintenance of their competitive position. Resources obtained in this market have helped cushion reserve pressures during restrictive periods of credit policy.

Until late 1964 liabilities to their overseas branches never exceeded $1 billion and until 1966 were held well below $2 billion. With the "credit crunch" in 1966 borrowings rose sharply to about

---

[1] See: J. G. Kvasnicka, "Eurodollars—An Important Source of Funds for American Banks," *Business Conditions,* Federal Reserve Bank of Chicago, June, 1969; Fred R. Klopstock, "Euro-dollars in the Liquidity and Reserve Management of U.S. Banks," *Monthly Review,* Federal Reserve Bank of New York, July, 1968; *The Financing of Business with Euro-Dollars,* Morgan Guaranty Trust Company, International Banking Division, September, 1967; Norris Johnson, *Euro-dollars in the New International Money Market,* First National City Bank, July, 1964; and Roy L. Reierson, *The Euro-Dollar Market,* Bankers Trust Co., July, 1964.

[2] International payments currently accomplished by cable transfer, as well as the dollar side of foreign exchange transactions, are now settled in clearing house funds. Proposals have been made to change the practice to settlement in Federal Funds. This change would make a substantial increase in the demand for Funds.

CHART X
FEDERAL FUNDS AND CALL EURO–DOLLAR
DEPOSIT RATES 1965–1969

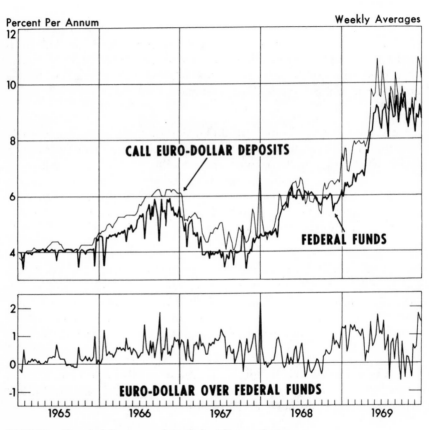

SOURCE: Board of Governors of the Federal Reserve System.

$4.3 billion. Accompanying the increasing credit demands and intensification of monetary restraint in late 1968, the level fluctuated around $15 billion throughout the fall of 1969, despite the imposition of reserve requirements against these liabilities in July and

October.[1] A number of banks without branches borrowed directly from overseas correspondents or through several of the U.S. security dealers who acted as brokers.

The Federal Reserve's easier monetary policy which had prevailed since early 1970 brought about a substantially lower level of money market rates. Since early summer, commercial banks had been able to issue a substantial volume of negotiable CD's and at the same time repay Euro-dollar borrowings. By mid-October some banks had reduced their reserve-free base, reflecting increasing confidence in the availability of money elsewhere at more favorable rates. Repayment of Euro-dollars resulted in excess holdings by foreign banks and accumulation of these dollars at foreign Central Banks.

In late November the System announced steps[2] to temper the repayment of Euro-dollars while avoiding penalty to banks that operate so as to retain their bases. The action was designed to restrict the size of the balance of payments deficit on official settlements basis.

---

[1]Effective July 31 member banks were required to count outstanding drafts or checks arising out of Euro-dollar transactions as demand deposits subject to reserve requirements. Euro-dollars were made more expensive when a 10 percent reserve requirement was imposed October 16 on any increase in liabilities to foreign branches over the daily average outstanding amounts in the four weeks ending May 28, 1969 (reserve-free base). The technical distinction between "deposits" and "due to branch" transformed Euro-dollar borrowing from a deposit liability subject to reserves into a reserve free liability until the imposition of reserves. Reserves were also imposed upon member bank borrowings from foreign correspondents. See Regulation D. For the banking system as a whole required reserves were reduced, excess reserves increased, and total reserves remained the same, although they supported a larger volume of earning assets.

[2]The Board raised from 10 to 20 percent the reserves required from member banks against Euro-dollar borrowings that exceed amounts that the banks are allowed as a reserve-free base. The higher requirement becomes effective in the four-week reserve computation period ending December 23.

To assure that banks that currently have Euro-dollar liabilities above their reserve-free bases are not penalized, the Board made the marginal reserve requirement applicable to borrowings above either (1) the minimum base equal to a percentage of deposits, or (2) the average level in the reserve computation period ended November 25, whichever is higher.

The Board also discouraged repayment of Euro-dollar liabilities by those banks that operate under a minimum base equal to 3 percent of their overall deposits subject to reserve requirements. The amendment will apply the automatic downward adjustment to reserve-free bases of the latter kind as well as of the former. This amendment becomes effective with the reserve computation period ending January 20, 1971.

The Board stated that this action was "deliberately made of modest scale." At the same time it was announced that other measures were being reviewed that might moderate repayment of Euro-dollars and avoid penalty to banks that retain their reserve-free bases.

As it has developed, the Euro-dollar market has contributed to fuller integration of money markets throughout Europe, as well as in Japan and the United States. It has also provided financing for expansion of world trade and investment. On the other hand, like other money markets but perhaps to a greater degree, the succession of short-term claims imposes risks. The liquidity of each participant is dependent to some extent upon the ability of ultimate borrowers to meet their obligations.

In contrast to these short-term money markets, which have evolved without official assistance, are those in Canada, Australia, South Africa, and India, which are developing with differing degrees of official encouragement and support.[1] They are designed to meet the needs of the particular institutional framework. But the purpose is the same — to achieve a more fully integrated financial system.

---

[1] See J. S. G. Wilson, "The New Money Markets," *Lloyds Bank Review*, No. 64, April, 1962.

Official Rulings Affecting the Funds Market

RULINGS OF THE BOARD OF GOVERNORS

Section 19 of the Federal Reserve Act makes possible borrowing and lending of excess member bank reserve balances or the purchases and sales of Funds. It reads in part:

"The required balance carried by a member bank with a Federal Reserve Bank may, under the regulations and subject to such penalties as may be prescribed by the Board of Governors of the Federal Reserve System, be checked against and withdrawn by such member banks for the purpose of meeting existing liabilities..."(12 U.S.C. 464.)

The market in Funds which grew out of this provision of the Act has been subject to several rulings by the Board. Two of these arose over the uncertainty and lack of uniformity in reporting Funds purchases and sales. The third involved sales of Funds between bank subsidiaries of a holding company. The fourth concerns a procedure for accomplishing sales of Funds by a member bank for a correspondent at its request through a transfer on the member bank's books from the deposit account of the correspondent to a bills payable or similar account. The transaction is carried out at the current rate for Funds. A fifth ruling concerned the scope of Funds trading by foreign banking corporations operating under the provisions of Regulation K, and the sixth restricted the use of repurchase agreements by banks with nonbanks.

Early in 1970, the Board issued amendments to its regulations which narrowed the category of Funds transactions which member banks may conduct and which may be classified as nondeposit borrowings rather than as deposits and consequently not subject to Regulations D and Q. It also harmonized regulations and interpretations concerning methods of effecting trades.

1. THE BOARD RULING OF SEPTEMBER, 1928. This ruling established that when a bank purchasing Funds gave its cashier's

check or authorized the selling bank to clear a ticket through the clearing house settlement on the day agreed upon, the liability created should be carried on the books of the bank buying Funds as "money borrowed." The amounts involved were to be reported under the account caption "Bills Payable and Rediscounts," rather than as a "Deposit Liability." The effect of this ruling was to exempt banks from including official checks used to return Funds in gross demand deposits in computing required reserves. These checks are commonly known as "bills payable checks." (1928 *Bulletin,* 656.) This ruling was withdrawn April, 1970 (See page 104.)

2. THE BOARD RULING OF JANUARY, 1930. When the practice of using book entries and wire transfers in settling transactions became widespread toward the end of the 1920's, the Board ruled that "all such transactions" should be classified in accordance with the purpose to be effected and the principles involved, rather than in accordance with the mechanics. On every such transaction — whether effected by check, book entry, wire transfer, or otherwise — and regardless of the method of repayment, the purchasing bank was required to show its resulting liability to the selling bank as money borrowed, and the selling bank was required to treat the transaction as a loan. In using the Board's Form 105 for report of condition, the purchasing member bank should show the liability incurred in any such transaction under "Bills Payable and Rediscounts," and the selling bank should enter the amounts under "Loans and Discounts." (1930 *Bulletin,* 81.)

By directing the banks to treat Funds sales as loans, the ruling limited the amount of Funds that national or state member banks could sell to individual borrowers, since Federal and most state statutes limit loans to a percentage of unimpaired capital and surplus. The provision that aggregate borrowing cannot exceed unimpaired capital and 50 percent of surplus imposed on national banks and similar requirements for many state banks were also limiting factors for purchases.

3. THE BOARD RULING OF JANUARY, 1959. As Funds trading became more widespread and holding company systems grew, the question arose whether "sales" of Funds at current rates of interest, "between bank subsidiaries of a holding company would constitute extensions of credit to a bank holding company of which

it is a subsidiary or to any other subsidiary of such bank holding company."

In reply, the Board stated that in accordance with its earlier ruling in 1930 and that of other supervisory authorities, such a "sale" would constitute a prohibited loan or extension of credit. It was also the Board's view that "sales" of Funds are not exempted from the prohibitions of Section 6(a) of the Bank Holding Company Act by the following provision of the last paragraph of that subsection: "Non-interest bearing deposits to the credit of a bank shall not be deemed to be a loan or advance to the bank of deposit...."The 1930 ruling had clearly indicated that funds transferred through the Funds market are not deposits in the "purchasing" bank. (12 CFR 222.110; 1959 *Bulletin*, 7.)

This 1959 ruling, however, was withdrawn by the Board upon the repeal by Congress, on July 1, 1966, of Section 6 of the Bank Holding Company Act. The change in the law, in effect, permitted the subsidiary banks of a bank holding company to deal with each other at arm's length. They are currently as free to trade Funds as are any other banks, within the limits and collateral requirements of Section 23A of the Federal Reserve Act.

4. THE BOARD RULING OF JULY, 1964. On July 27, 1964, the Board replied to an inquiry from a member bank regarding the procedure whereby a bank requests its correspondent to "invest for a certain period of time" — overnight or for a few days or weeks — a specified portion of the bank's deposit balance with the correspondent, and the correspondent itself agrees to "borrow these funds...at the Federal Funds rate." The Board stated that the specified amount could be transferred on the books of the correspondent from the deposit account to "Bills Payable" and interest paid at the rate currently paid for Federal Funds. (12 CFR 217.137; 1964 *Bulletin*, 1000; Published *Interpretations*, Paragraph 3261.)

It was pointed out that the right of a member bank to "purchase" (borrow) Federal Funds from other banks has never been questioned, and the seller of such Funds may be either a member or nonmember that is in a position to arrange for Funds to be transferred to the "purchaser" from a member bank's Federal Reserve deposit account.

The Board stated that it was unable to find any basis on which to distinguish similar transactions when the Funds to be borrowed are on deposit in the "purchasing" bank. If such a distinction were drawn, the "selling" bank could read..y have the Funds transferrred to its account in a third bank and then have the same amount transferred back to the borrowing bank by entries on the books of the Federal Reserve bank.

It was further stated that the prohibitions of Section 19 of the Federal Reserve Act and those of Regulation Q relate only to the payment of interest on demand deposits. It does not prohibit the payment of interest on "borrowed money" by member banks in circumstances as outlined in the ruling.

A ruling effective February 12, 1970, amended this interpretation so that *nonbank intrabank transfers* from deposit account to borrowed money account and payment of interest thereon were prohibited. (1970 *Bulletin*, 38-39; and also see p.103, Board Ruling No. 7.) Such transactions for the banks' corporate customers had increased significantly after the 1964 ruling and were not considered good banking practice.

5. THE BOARD RULING OF NOVEMBER, 1964. This ruling permitted foreign banking corporations operating under the provisions of Regulation K to purchase or sell Funds to adjust their reserve balances at Federal Reserve banks. Transactions for regular investment were not allowed. Funds sold by the corporation must be included in loans subject to the limitations and restrictions in section 211.9(b) of Regulation K. Funds bought must be treated as liabilities for borrowed money. (12 CFR 211.101; 1964 *Bulletin*, 1414; Published *Interpretations*, Paragraph 5700.)

The revision of Regulation K in 1957 was followed by a renewed interest in foreign banking corporations, and as international trade expanded, a number of these corporations have been chartered.

6. THE BOARD RULING OF JULY, 1969. For some time, market observers had felt that repurchase agreements offered member banks a major loophole for evading regulations concerning deposits and, in particular, payment of interest on demand deposits.

A number of banks were using such instruments with U.S. securities, loans, municipal securities, and CD's as collateral in connection with Funds transactions with nonbanks and also to procure funds for longer periods. Consequently, the Board decided to restrain their use.

Beginning August 28, 1969, every bank liability on a repurchase agreement entered into on or after July 25, 1969, with a person other than a bank and involving assets other than direct obligations of the United States or its agencies (and obligations guaranteed by them) was ruled to be a deposit. Repurchase agreements collateraled with U.S. securities and agencies made by banks with nonbanks were excepted from classification as deposits largely to permit dealer banks to help finance inventories of U.S. securities.

A repurchase agreement with a person other than a bank with respect to a part interest in *any* obligation or obligations, including U.S. Government securities, was also prohibited. An amendment effective August 15, 1969, however, continued to permit transactions involving a part interest in an obligation eligible for Federal Reserve purchase and to classify the liability thereon as a nondeposit borrowing. (12 CFR 204.1(f); 1969 *Bulletin*, 655, 736.)

7. THE BOARD RULING OF FEBRUARY, 1970. This ruling effective February 12, 1970, narrowed the category of Funds transactions permitted member banks. Its chief objective was to prohibit transactions by member banks with certain nonbanks. The term bank is defined in this ruling to include a member bank, a nonmember commercial bank, a savings bank, a building or savings and loan association, a cooperative bank, the Export-Import Bank of the United States, or a foreign bank. It also included bank subsidiaries that engage in business in which the parents are authorized to engage and subsidiaries the stock of which is by statute explicitly eligible for purchases by national banks. Foreign banking corporations operating under the provisions of Regulation K are such a class of corporation.

Currently four classes of Funds purchases and other short-term borrowings by member banks are considered nondeposit funds and are excluded from the provisions of Regulations D and Q.

1. Borrowings from other banks. These transactions are considered necessary for the efficient functioning of the Funds market, which is believed to be useful in effecting monetary policy.

2. Repurchase transactions in U.S. securities and Federal agency securities eligible for Federal Reserve purchase.

3. Funds borrowings from security dealers arising from the clearance of securities. This type of transaction, in conjunction with No. 2, aids the effective function of U.S. financial markets.

4. Borrowings by member banks from various governmental institutions.

In order to assure that the exemption for liabilities to banks is not used as a means by which nonbanks may arrange to sell Funds to a member bank, obligations within the exception must be issued to another bank for its own account. Consequently, banks should take action necessary to ascertain the character of the seller in order to justify the classification of its liability for the transaction as Funds purchased rather than as a deposit. (12 CFR 204.1(f); 1970 *Bulletin*, 37–38.)

On July 1, 1970, the Board denied a request from a trust company engaged solely in trust business to modify Regulations D and Q so that it would be permitted to sell Funds to a member bank. The Board stated that expansion of the interbank liability to permit a member bank to purchase Funds from a trust company would be inconsistent with the policy on access to the market. It was argued that even if a trust company were considered a "bank," sales of Funds by it are not for its own account but rather for the account of beneficiaries of the trusts, a category that includes invididuals and corporations.

8. THE BOARD RULING OF APRIL, 1970. The 1928 ruling in effect exempted a bank from the requirement that all officers' checks issued by a member bank be included in its gross demand deposits for reserve purposes. The receiving bank could, of course, deduct all cash items in the process of collection from its gross

demand deposits in establishing its reserve requirements. Permitting both the issuing and receiving banks an exclusion from their respective deposit liabilities was considered to be inconsistent with the basis of the provision for cash-item deductions, which was instituted to avoid situations in which two member banks maintain reserves against the same funds. Instead, such a deduction would result in neither bank maintaining reserves against such funds. It is understood that it was never general practice for banks engaging in Federal Funds transactions to deduct checks received in payment from their deposits in reserve computation, despite the consistency of such a deduction with the language of the regulation.

A survey by the Reserve System in early 1970 found that almost all Funds transactions are currently handled through entries on the books of the Reserve banks. Accordingly, the 1928 ruling was withdrawn on April 2, 1970. Henceforth, Funds transactions between banks will be settled by book entry at the Federal Reserve banks in lieu of officers' checks. (1970 *Bulletin,* 280.)

RULINGS OF THE COMPTROLLER OF THE CURRENCY

Until September, 1956, "repurchase agreements" were viewed as not being subject to the legal loan or borrowing limits of national or state member banks. In general, they were treated as investments. The securities involved in the transactions included U.S. Government securities, certain agency issues, such as public housing authority bonds, and at times, municipal bonds. Most frequently, the U.S. Government securities underlying the transactions were short-term, but on occasion, intermediate and longer term issues were involved. In recent years, however, the Comptroller of the Currency has issued rulings which required these transactions to be regarded as loans or borrowings, set certain limits on the amounts of individual transactions, and which specified the underlying securities.

1. THE COMPTROLLER'S RULINGS, 1956 and 1957. On September 14, 1956, the Comptroller issued a ruling that had a limiting effect on sales or purchases of Funds when accomplished through repurchase agreements. These transactions, defined as loans or borrowings, were brought within the scope of Sections 5200 and 5202, U.S.R.S. Sales of Funds in this form were limited to 25

percent of capital and surplus of a member bank. After some discussion and consideration of the nature and purpose of these transactions, the Comptroller held the limitation was inapplicable if the transactions occurred between a member bank and a Government securities dealer or broker. This ruling was issued on January 28, 1957. One of the effects of this ruling was to place nonbank Government securities dealers in a preferred position in accomplishing repurchase agreements or buy backs, compared with transactions between national or state member banks.

After further consideration of the use of repurchase agreements and related types of transactions in financing Government securities dealers or in exchanging Funds, the Comptroller ruled that effective August 16, 1957, the obligations of any member bank in the form notes of any person, co-partnership, association, or corporation, secured by not less than a like amount of *direct* obligations of the United States, which will mature in a period not exceeding 18 months from the date of such obligations to such member bank, shall be limited to the amount of capital and surplus of the member bank. This ruling eliminated the use of longer term U.S. Government securities and agency issues in transactions involving the maximum limit for such types of Funds transactions.

U.S. Government securities maturing in over 18 months and agency obligations involved in an individual transaction were subject to the limit of 25 percent of a member bank's capital and surplus. Repurchase agreements involving municipal securities were subject to the 10 percent limit on individual loans.

After the effective date of the regulations, member banks in reporting repurchase transactions on the Call Reports showed them as loans for the purpose of purchasing or carrying securities, rather than being included with securities owned. The selling (borrowing) bank continued to report such transactions as borrowings and continued to report the securities as owned. Borrowing limits were not changed by these rulings.

Subsequently, as the market became aware of the rulings, a number of protests were made by both nonbank Government security dealers and banking institutions. In summary, they contended that the rulings made it more costly and difficult for

Government security dealers to finance portfolios, hindering the dealers in attempting to make the broadest markets; banks outside New York City found it more difficult to invest temporary funds readily and efficiently. The banks also complained about the necessity for entering into arrangements with several borrowers or buyers instead of one because of the added accounting detail and increase in overhead costs. The effects were reported to be felt more keenly in periods of tight money. Others pointed out that repurchase agreements involved less risk to the purchaser than did outright acquisitions, and, thus, there was no reason to limit them in amount beyond the requirements of Section 5136 of the Revised Statutes. It was further argued that repurchase agreements also made it possible for short-term investors to acquire desired maturities not otherwise available in the market.

From the point of view of the Federal Reserve, repurchases were an important money market instrument for effecting policy. They helped to facilitate the mobilization and distribution of available reserves through the Government securities market.

The Comptroller was unwilling to recognize the argument for treating repurchases as investment securities transactions under Section 5136 of the Revised Statutes. He also dismissed the suggestion of some market participants that repurchases involving securities not exceeding 18 months in maturity be exempted from the loan category and that, as a matter of supervisory jurisdiction, such transactions be reported separately under such definition as the Comptroller, by regulation, may describe.

2. THE COMPTROLLER'S RULING, 1958. A new regulation, effective April 18, 1958, reflected a compromise. It exempted from the limitations based upon capital and surplus of national banking associations, obligations to any such associations secured by not less than a like amount of "direct obligations of the United States which will mature in not exceeding 18 months from the date of entering such obligations to such national banking associations." The exception provided by this ruling dispelled the confusion existing in the market, and the volume of activity expanded further.

3. THE COMPTROLLER'S RULING, 1963. On June 1, 1963, a new *Manual for National Banks* containing a series of rulings

concerning bank practice was published by the Comptroller. Among the interpretations dealing with obligations subject to lending limits was Paragraph 1130 of the rulings concerning Federal Funds:

"When a bank purchases federal reserve Funds from another bank, the transaction ordinarily takes the form of a transfer from a seller's account in a Federal Reserve Bank to the buyer's account therein, payment to be made by the purchaser, usually with a specified fee. The transaction does not create on the part of the buyer an obligation subject to 12 U.S.C. 84 or a borrowing subject to 12 U.S.C. 82, but is to be considered a purchase and sale of such funds."

The ruling reversed the previous position of the Comptroller's office and held that such transactions by national banks do not constitute loans within the limitations of Section 5200 or borrowings within the limitations of Section 5202 of the Revised Statutes. No reasons have been given for the ruling. Several state banking officials were reported as stating that the ruling is another effort by the Comptroller to give national banks an advantage over state banks. Other observers criticized the ruling as a lowering of the "reasonableness and good sense of bank supervision."

On September 9, 1963, the Board of Governors stated that it continued to be its position that, for purposes of provisions of law administered by the Board, a transaction in Federal Funds involves a loan on the part of the selling bank and a borrowing on the part of the purchasing bank.

The Board reaffirmed its earlier position that for the purposes of Section 23A of the Federal Reserve Act, which had been added by the Banking Act of 1933, a sale of Federal Funds by a member bank, whether state or national, to an affiliate of the member bank, is subject to the limitations prescribed in that section. Similarly, the Board reaffirmed a January, 1959, ruling that a sale of Federal Funds by a banking subsidiary or bank in the same holding company system would result in a criminal violation of the provisions of Section 6 of the Bank Holding Company Act of 1956 (repealed, June, 1966; see page 101.)

4. THE COMPTROLLER'S RULING, 1964. On March 31, 1964, the Comptroller in effect rescinded his earlier ruling on

repurchase agreements. Paragraph 1131 was added to the list of interpretations in the *Manual for National Banks* as follows:

"The purchase or sale of securities by a bank, under an agreement to resell or repurchase at the end of a stated period, is not a borrowing subject to 12 U.S.C. 82 nor an obligation subject to the lending limit of 12 U.S.C. 84."

This ruling places repurchase agreements on the same basis as direct Funds transactions. Since the Comptroller's rulings, some national banks have been reported as more willing to enter into transactions of a modestly larger size, particularly on the selling side. However, observers state that there has been little overall change in total Funds activity that can be attributed to the ruling. The major change reported is a reduction in the use of securities to collateralize Funds purchased from banks with relatively small lending limits. Perhaps more than half of the transactions that were previously required to be secured have been freed or the amount of collateral reduced. Accommodating banks, in dealing with correspondents, have generally continued to trade within previously agreed lines, and, in those instances where limits are increased, they have taken a closer look at the credit standing of the correspondent. Departure from the old limits, when it occurs, is generally on the sales side. A number of smaller banks, however, have been encouraged to enter the market. Borrowing proportions continue generally as before, with an occasional report of a bank attempting to exploit several lenders.

These rulings have probably resulted in encouraging a modest increase in total Funds activity and helped to further concentration in trading activity in the large banks on the demand side. Most banks have generally observed or remained close to conventional limits.

In compliance with these rulings, national banks will report Funds purchases and sales under a caption so designated on the Call Report.

Some state supervisors have given informal approval to state banks, when permissible under prevailing statutes, to trade on the same basis as national banks. In those states where the law was more restrictive and needed amendment, the state banks may have been placed in an unfair competitive position.

Appendix B

Some Definitions and the Mechanics of Transactions in Federal Funds

FEDERAL FUNDS

This term is shorthand for "immediately available Federal Reserve Funds" and means, essentially, title to reserve balances (of member banks) at Federal Reserve banks. In earlier periods of the market, the principal means of transferring titles to reserve balances was checks. The selling bank issued a check drawn on the Federal Reserve, and the buying bank returned the Funds with an official clearing house check. The Federal Reserve check was collectible upon presentation at the Reserve bank in immediately available Funds. The check on a clearing house bank was collectible in Funds available at the Reserve bank the next day when clearing balances were settled on the books of the Reserve bank.

Since April 2, 1970, clearing house checks cannot be used by the member bank buyer to return Funds to the seller (see p. 104, Board Ruling No. 8, April, 1970). Transfers are now made by entries on the books of the Reserve banks in response to telephone, teletypewriter, or telegraph instruction of the selling and buying bank.

Title to Federal Funds may also be acquired through checks issued by the U.S. Treasury, certain clearing nonmember banks, foreign official banks when drawn against their balances at the Reserve banks, and by Reserve System disbursing officers.

Using the Federal Reserve wire transfer facilities, a bank may wire Federal Funds to other banks in different localities for their own use or that of their customers. Funds for wire transmission come from the sending bank's reserve account, and the proceeds at the other end flow into the receiving bank's reserve account.

No interest is paid by the Reserve banks on balances held with them. Consideration of profit dictates that member banks continuously employ any surplus reserves in interest-earning outlets. Thus, Federal Funds sales is one of several alternatives in the money market for investment of temporary excess reserves. A conventional Funds sale of $1 million for one day (overnight lending) would return the seller $166.667 if Funds are trading at 6 percent. The Funds rate is determined by the day's trading and is figured on a 360-day basis. If sold on Friday—over the weekend—the return would be $500.00 since the next clearing is three days away.

UNITS OF TRADING AND TYPES OF TRANSACTIONS

The common unit of trading is $1 million, although at times transactions are accomplished in blocks of $200,000 or large multiples under $1 million. Some liberalization of trading units has developed in recent years as a result of competition among the accommodating banks. Minimum trades in accommodating arrangements range in size from $200,000 down to $25,000 and even $10,000, on occasion, in some districts. Most frequently, however, the trading unit is between $50,000 and $200,000 in size.

Until the ruling of the Comptroller in 1963, Funds sales were considered unsecured loans made by one bank to another. They came under the single borrower limitation for unsecured loans in the National Bank Act, and individual transactions were limited to 10 percent of capital and surplus. There are similar limitations in many state statutes. The provision imposed on national banks and many state banks stipulating that aggregate borrowings cannot exceed capital stock and a percentage of surplus also limited purchases.

Thus, direct trades of Funds in size were generally confined to the larger banks. During the 1950's, however, the smaller banks developed the practice of using repurchase agreements, buy backs, or general U.S. Government short-term security collateral transactions to enter the Funds market on the selling side. The common unit for accomplishing these transactions is also $1 million.

Until 1957, these secured transactions were carried in the bank's investment account and were considered investment transactions to avoid the loan limits. Rulings of the Comptroller in 1957 and 1958 required such transactions to be classified as loans by national banks and permitted certain exceptions from the limits when secured by U.S. Government securities. State member banks met similar conditions. The ruling of the Comptroller in June, 1963, however, freed all Funds transactions of national banks from lending and borrowing limits. Market practice, however, generally continues to observe the old regulations in amount of transactions, but there has been a reduction in the number of collateral transactions, especially in tight markets.

REPURCHASE AGREEMENTS, OR BUY BACKS, WITH DEALERS

These terms are practically synonymous and in their more technical usage are applied to transactions by which a bank makes a firm purchase of Government securities for delivery and payment in Federal Funds the same day. Concurrently, the bank makes a firm sale with the same dealer of the same amount of the same issue of Government securities for delivery and payment in Federal Funds on the following business day at an agreed price.

The transaction prices are usually at or below the bid side of the market. Most commonly the dealer sells the securities to the customer at an agreed price, flat, and buys them back at the same price, flat. The customer receives a rate of interest on the contract based on par value or one related to the market.

In other instances, the securities are sold to the customer at an agreed rate of intest and repurchased at the same rate, or, the dealer may sell them to the customer at market and accrued interest and buy them back at a price which will provide an agreed yield. Written confirmations of the sale and purchase are delivered, and the payments in Federal Funds are made on the respective settlement dates. Less frequently, banks may borrow Funds from banks or dealers in an analogous transaction known as a "reverse repurchase." The volume of these transactions, however, is usually relatively small.

During the severely restrictive periods of credit restraint in 1966 and 1969, however, the banks became quite active in making reverse repurchases in order to conserve their holdings of U.S. securities. By entering into these agreements with dealers, the securities are used as a basis for borrowing from the dealer. The dealer finds the money from nonbank sources by entering into a repurchase with a nonbank. The two transactions ordinarily have the same maturity and are equal in amount, thus canceling out. Market estimates place the volume of transactions at about $1 billion daily during much of 1969. Dealers are generally compensated for their services with a one-quarter to three-eighths of a point spread depending in some degree on maturity. These transactions may also be undertaken to satisfy a corporate customer who needs cash but does not wish to disturb his portfolio.

Repurchase agreements are generally made for overnight, but they may be "open," particularly when they arise between a dealer and a bank and run for two or three days; the exact period being indeterminate when initiated. Some provide automatic renewal until terminated. The parties to the transaction usually agree to ignore the coupon rate on the securities and the yield to maturity. The specified rate is related to the going rate on Federal Funds, the dealer loan rate in New York, and, to a lesser extent, the Treasury bill rate. If the transaction is "open," the rate is set from day to day as noted earlier. During the tight money market of 1969, however, dealers at times were able to make repurchases with certain nonbanks at a level between the Funds rate and discount rate. Usually it was close to the commercial paper rate. Shortage of collateral or desire to conserve holdings of U.S. securities on the part of banks and dealer willingness and need to carry inventory were among the factors responsible for this development.

Repurchases may provide automatic adjustment of the rate to the market, and some agreements may permit substitution of collateral. The use of these transactions between banks, and between banks and dealers, varies. Overnight transactions between dealers and banks outside New York City have been widespread and also occur between dealer banks in New York and out-of-town banks. More generally, secured interbank Funds transactions do not involve the precise pricing of securities as is characteristic of repurchases with dealers.

If the transactions originate between a bank and a dealer's office outside New York, the tickets are billed to the local office, but settlement is made in New York for their accounts. Virtually all of

113

these transactions outside New York are accomplished by wire transfer, with debits and credits of Federal Funds to correspondent account balances maintained in New York City. The instructions to pay the Funds to the borrower against delivery of the securities flow over the "bank wire." The securities involved in the transaction are held in safekeeping accounts in New York.

ACCOMMODATING BANKS AND CORRESPONDENT TRADING ARRANGEMENTS

Accommodating banks buy and sell Funds to meet their own reserve needs but, in addition, provide or absorb Funds as a service to correspondent banks and others.

Some lead correspondents have taken an aggressive approach in developing outright limited trading positions in Funds to enable them to provide a "new business service," selling or buying Funds to or from their correspondents, while others encourage only sales. Reluctant to improve the familiarity of smaller banks with the market, a few have adopted a passive attitude by offering a service of buying or selling only upon request from the smaller banks. The largest accommodating banks usually operate on both sides of the market during the same day.

In providing or absorbing Funds as a service to correspondents, the accommodator generally will:

1. match — on its own books, to the extent possible — buy and sell orders from correspondent or customer banks;

2. care for the correspondent's needs out of its own position when its reserve position is the reverse of its correspondent's;

3. try its best to cover a correspondent's needs in the national market when it can't accomplish transactions by (1) or (2).

At times, the accommodator may borrow from the Federal Reserve bank. In other cases, the lead correspondent acts only as agent, pooling sales of a customer's bank with his own. Purchases by smaller banks come from the lead bank's position.

All of the accommodating or corresponent arrangements do not provide the same degree of service, and some may limit their service at certain times during the year or depending on conditions in the market. In some cases, a collateral loan agreement may be required of the correspondent. When the service provides for purchases by the smaller banks, the lead bank usually sets up an informal "line of Funds." If the correspondent wants to borrow more, the request is referred to an officer in charge of the money position or the representative who regularly calls upon the particular bank.

Correspondent charges on purchases and sales vary. Some accommodators may make a charge on purchases but sell at the prevailing rate regardless of the amount. Others will make a charge on sales. Charges usually vary with the size of the trade. On amounts under $1 million, the spread may be one-half of 1 percent and over $1 million, one-eighth to one-quarter of 1 percent. The spread between buying and selling, however, widened at times in many city and regional trading arrangements as rates became more volatile in the 1969 money market. The widened spread offered more protection against loss. If acting as agent or if sales are combined with those of the accommodator, the correspondent receives the rate on the combined transaction. Few if any of the large banks view Funds as a direct source of profits.

A very small profit or loss in their purchases from and sales to customers may arise from rate fluctuations during the day. In some banks the Funds are traded even (a good 8 percent market would mean a bid in size at 8 percent and an offering in size at 8 percent). More banks may return to "even trades" as the hyperactivity of recent markets moderates. Profits in this instance may come from differences in rates during the reserve period, selling at 8 percent early in the period in hope of buying them at a lower rate at the end of the period.

Probably 85 percent of the transactions are for overnight, and the rest range from three days to two weeks, with the rate fixed from day to day. In some instances, Funds remain at the bank's disposal until either party terminates the arrangement or until the rate changes. There has been a tendency to increase the length of transactions with smaller banks.

In contrast to the accommodating banks, the other regular participants usually come into the market on only one side, either borrowing or selling, on a particular day unless their money position undergoes a market swing during the day. Over time, they tend to be net buyers or net sellers.

The number of banks involved in these arrangements range from five or six to several hundred. To a considerable extent these networks are mutually exclusive.

MARKET RULES

Selling banks may impose their own limits on borrowing banks and may restrict their transactions to banks on an approved list. Some banks which view the market on an impersonal basis may develop their lists without reference to correspondent relationships but will honor direct requests from correspondents for purchases if Funds are available in their position. The list of banks with which another bank may deal may be more closely observed in tight markets than when they are easier.

MECHANICS OF ACCOMPLISHING TRANSACTIONS

1. INTRACITY. Among banks within a city, transactions in buying or selling Funds are made by telephone between borrowing and lending banks and may be initiated by either one. The lending bank then telephones the Federal Reserve bank to charge its account and credit the borrowing bank. The call to the Reserve bank is followed by letter or teletypewriter instructions to the Reserve bank, and the buyer makes written confirmation to the seller. The entries are reversed the next day by the buying bank. Interest is handled separately by a charge or credit to correspondent accounts or by treasurer's or cashier's check.

In a few cities until the spring of 1970, local transactions were still accomplished by the selling bank's check on the Federal Reserve bank, and the transaction was discharged by the borrower's clearing house check plus one day's interest at an agreed rate. Until 1961, this was also the practice in New York. Under an agreement by the New York Clearing House banks in 1966, the issuance of the clearing house check by the buyer was enough acknowledgment, and the seller no longer issued a check but merely instructed the Reserve bank by telephone to charge its account and credit the buyer. Generally, the New York City banks do not arrange transactions directly with one another; instead they use the brokers as intermediaries.

2. INTRADISTRICT. Transactions arranged between banks in different cities within a district are usually accomplished by telephone instruction to the Reserve bank, both in opening and closing. The transaction may be arranged by a broker or through direct communication from one bank to another by telephone or the commercial bank wire. Letter or teletypewriter instruction follow the telephone calls to the Reserve bank, and the transaction is confirmed in writing to the seller by the buyer. Interest is charged or credited to correspondent accounts or settled by an official check.

3. INTERDISTRICT. The lending bank instructs the Federal Reserve by telephone, or teletypewriter to wire Funds to the borrowing bank in another district for immediate payment, and the borrower repays the loan with a return wire of Funds on the following business day. The buying bank normally confirms the transaction to the seller by both telegram and letter. Interest is settled by credit or charge to correspondent accounts or flows back by draft or check if no correspondent relationship is involved. This practice is usually followed because the Federal Reserve charges for wires involving odd sums.

FUNDS BROKERS

Two member firms of the New York Stock Exchange, The Garvin Bantel Corp. and Mabon, Nugent & Co.; a New York commercial bank, Irving Trust Company; and an institutional money broker, George Palumbo & Co., Inc., maintain desks in regular daily contact with both buyers and sellers of Funds. None of these organizations deal as principals. They match purchases and sales orders received from banks desiring to use their services.

For its services, The Garvin Bantel Corp. is compensated by stock exchange business which it may receive. The firm also offers the banks a broker's loan facility when it suits the banks' loan needs.

At the request of a bank, a commission of one-sixteenth of 1 percent may be charged.

Mabon, Nugent & Co. may charge the banks a one-sixteenth of 1 percent commission in return for its services. As an alternative, the firm may receive stock exchange business.

The Funds brokerage service offered by Irving Trust Company is separate and independent of any other transactions which the bank may conduct in Funds. The service is supplied at no charge, but the bank may, through the offer of this service, receive other business from the customer banks.

George Palumbo & Co., Inc., in return for its services, may charge the banks a one-sixteenth of 1 percent commission. As an alternative, the firm may be compensated indirectly through referral of stock exchange business to member firms. A broker's loan service is offered as well.

ACKNOWLEDGMENTS

In the preparation of the first edition of this booklet, acknowledgment was made to persons who supplied information or discussed various parts of the paper. The author is particularly indebted to Herbert Repp and Robert Coon, Discount Corporation; L. M. Maxson, The First Boston Corporation; Girard Spencer, Salomon Brothers & Hutzler; Henry J. Schuler, The Bank of New York; George Garvin, The Garvin Bantel Corp.; Sumner Pruyne, The First National Bank of Boston; James Arrington, The National Shawmut Bank of Boston; and Randolph Flather, Industrial National Bank of Rhode Island, all now retired. Also, Richard Youndahl, Aubrey G. Lanston and Co., Inc.; Ralph DePaola, Mabon, Nugent & Co.; James Wilson and John Benson, The National Shawmut Bank of Boston; and John J. Cummings, Jr., Industrial National Bank of Rhode Island. A number of these same persons were also helpful with materials incorporated in the revised editions.

In the preparation of later editions, however, the author is indebted to Marshall Montgomery, Aubrey G. Lanston and Co., Inc.; Frederick Gidge (retired), Manufacturers Hanover Trust Company; Richard J. Chouinard, Irving Trust Company; Richard C. Fieldhouse, The Garvin Bantel Corp.; Lewis N. Dembitz, Carter H. Golembe Associates; John J. Arena, Loomis-Sayles & Company; Professor Donald R. Hodgman, University of Illinois; Irving Auerbach, Federal Reserve Bank of New York; Clay Anderson (retired), Federal Reserve Bank of Philadelphia; and Paul S. Anderson, Federal Reserve Bank of Boston.

The author alone is responsible for statements of fact and the conclusions in the text.

BIBLIOGRAPHY

Books

Beckhart, Benjamin H., and Smith, James G. *The New York Money Market*. Vol. II: *Sources and Movements of Funds*. New York: Columbia University Press, 1932.

Burgess, W. Randolph. *The Reserve Banks and the Money Market*. New York: Harper & Brothers, 1936.

Clark, Lawrence E. *Central Banking Under the Federal Reserve System*. New York: The Macmillan Company, 1935.

Crosse, Howard D. *Management Policies for Commercial Banks*. Englewood Cliffs, New Jersey: Prentice-Hall, Inc., 1962.

Fieldhouse, Richard C. *Certificates of Deposit*. Boston: The Bankers Publishing Company, 1962.

Madden, John T., and Nadler, Marcus. *The International Money Markets*. New York: Prentice-Hall, Inc., 1935.

Nadler, Marcus; Heller, Sipa; and Shipman, Samuel S. *The Money Market and Its Institutions*. New York: Ronald Press Company, 1955.

Robinson, Roland I., ed. *Financial Institutions*. Homewood, Illinois: Richard D. Irwin, Inc., 1960.

_____. *Money and Capital Markets*. New York: McGraw-Hill, 1964.

Sayers, Richard S. *Central Banking After Bagehot*. Oxford: Clarendon Press, 1957.

Selden, Richard T. *Trends and Cycles in the Commercial Paper Market*. (Occasional Paper No. 85.) New York: National Bureau of Economic Research, 1963.

Turner, Bernice C. *The Federal Fund Market.* New York: Prentice-Hall, Inc., 1931.

Westerfield, Ray B. *Money, Credit and Banking.* Revised ed. New York: Ronald Press Company, 1947.

Willis, Parker B. *The Federal Reserve Bank of San Francisco.* New York: Columbia University Press, 1937.

Articles and Periodicals

Bailly-Blancard, Arthur, "Buying and Selling Federal Funds and 'R.P.'s' are New Money Mart." *American Banker,* September 16, 1955, p.1ff.

Brophy, Charles. "Bill Snagging Ahead? Funds Always Over 3½%." *Weekly Bond Buyer,* June 15, 1964, p. 2.

Cowan, Edward. "Banks Deal Increasingly in Excess Federal Reserves." *New York Times,* October 17, 1963, pp. 49, 51.

Elliot, John. "Broker House Settles Loans Among Banks." *New York Herald Tribune,* February 25, 1951, Sec. II, p. 9.

Gidge, Frederick. "Billion Dollar Specialty: Security Dealer Clearance." *Burroughs Clearing House,* August, 1964, pp. 45-48.

Hambelton, James R. "Small Banks Push for Federal Fund Regional Markets.*" American Banker,* January 20, 1964, pp. 1ff.

————, and Benson, Michael. "Federal Funds Exempted from National Bank Lending Limits." *American Banker,* August 26, 1963, pp. 1, 3.

————. "Surprised Fed Voices Opposition to Saxon Federal Funds Ruling." *American Banker,* August 27, 1963, pp. 1ff.

Jacobs, Donald P. "The Marketable Security Portfolios of Non-financial Corporations, Investment Practices and Trends." *Journal of Finance,* XV (September, 1960), 341-352.

Minsky, Hyman P. "Central Banking and Money Market Change." *Quarterly Journal of Economics,* LXXI (May, 1957), 188-205.

"New Settlement Arrangements for Member Banks." *The Morgan Guaranty Survey,* Morgan Guaranty Trust Company (May, 1968), pp. 3-5.

Olsen, Leif H. "From Bank to Bank." *New York Times,* September 23, 1956.

Silberman, Charles E. "The Big Corporate Lenders." *Fortune,* August, 1956, pp. 111ff.

Stone, Robert W. "The Changing Structure of the Money Market." *The Journal of Finance,* XX (May, 1965), 229-38.

Tyng, Ed. "Federal Funds Deals Rise." *Journal of Commerce,* September 7, 1951.

Wilson, J. S. G. "America's Changing Bank Scene: III. The Money Market." *The Banker,* CVII (June, 1957), 394-401.

_____. "The New Money Markets." *Lloyds Bank Review,* No. 64 (April, 1962), 31-45.

_____. "The Structure of Money Markets." *Banca Nazionale del Lavoro Quarterly Review,* No. 56 (March, 1961).

Publications of the Federal Reserve System

Board of Governors of the Federal Reserve System. *Annual Report.* Washington: Board of Governors, 1952-1969.

_____. *The Federal Funds Market -- A Study by a Federal Reserve System Committee.* Washington: Board of Governors, 1959.

_____. *The Federal Reserve System: Purposes and Functions.* 5th ed. Washington: Board of Governors, 1963.

————. "New Series on Federal Funds." *Federal Reserve Bulletin.* August, 1964, pp. 944-74.

————. *Reappraisal of the Federal Reserve Discount Mechanism: Report of a System Committee.* Washington: Board of Governors, July, 1968.

Brandt, Harry, and Crowe, Paul A. "The Federal Funds Market in the Southeast." *Monthly Review,* Federal Reserve Bank of Atlanta, (January, 1968), pp. 7-13.

————, and Wyand, Robert R. II. "Using a Sharper Pencil?" Part I. *Monthly Review,* Federal Reserve Bank of Atlanta (November, 1965), pp. 1-4.

Cacy, J. A. "Tenth District Banks in the Federal Funds Market." *Monthly Review,* Federal Reserve Bank of Kansas City (November, 1969), pp. 10-20.

Carr, Hobart C. "Federal Funds." *Money Market Essays.* New York: Federal Reserve Bank of New York, March, 1950, pp. 13-16.

Colby, William G., Jr., and Platt, Robert B. "Second District 'Country' Member Banks in the Federal Funds Market." *Monthly Review,* Federal Reserve Bank of New York (May, 1966), pp. 114-18.

Crowe, Paul A., and Wyand, Robert R. II. "Using a Sharper Pencil?" Part II. *Monthly Review,* Federal Reserve Bank of Atlanta (December, 1965), pp. 1-4.

Duprey, J. N. "Country Bank Participation in the Federal Funds Market." *Monthly Review,* Federal Reserve Bank of Minneapolis (July, 1966), pp. 3-8.

"Federal Funds." *Monthly Review of Credit and Business Conditions,* Federal Reserve Bank of New York (March, 1950), pp. 28-30.

"Federal Funds in Fifth District." *Monthly Review,* Federal Reserve Bank of Richmond (June, 1961), pp. 8-10 and (September, 1966), pp. 8-11.

Federal Reserve Bank of Chicago. *Midwest Banking in the Sixties -- A Decade of Growth and Change.*Chicago: Federal Feserve Bank of Chicago, March, 1970.

Federal Reserve Bank of New York. *Annual Report.* 1924.

Freeman, Louise. "The Financing of Government Security Dealers." *Monthly Review,* Federal Reserve Bank of New York (June, 1964), pp. 107-16.

Griggs, William N. "Federal Funds Market in the Southwest." *Business Review,* Federal Reserve Bank of Dallas (November, 1961), pp. 1-6.

Hirsch, Albert A. "Adjusting Reserves Through the Federal Funds Market. The Record of District Banks." *Monthly Review,* Federal Reserve Bank of Atlanta (October, 1962), pp. 1-3.

Holmes, Alan R., and Klopstock, Fred R. "The Market for Dollar Deposits in Europe." *Monthly Review,* Federal Reserve Bank of New York (November, 1960), pp. 197-202.

Klopstock, Fred R. "Euro-dollar in the Liquidity and Reserve Management of U. S. Banks." *Monthly Review,* Federal Reserve Bank of New York (July, 1968), pp. 130-38.

Kvasnicka, J. G. "Eurodollars -- An Important Source of Funds for American Banks." *Business Conditions,* Federal Reserve Bank of Chicago (June, 1969), pp. 9-20.

Madden, Carl H. *The Money Side of "The Street."* New York: Federal Reserve Bank of New York, 1959.

Monhollon, Jimmie R., ed. *Instruments of the Money Market.* Richmond: Federal Reserve Bank of Richmond, February, 1968.

Nichols, Dorothy M. "Federal Funds, How Banks Use the Market." *Business Conditions,* Federal Reserve Bank of Chicago (October, 1967), pp. 2-11.

————. "Marketing Money: How 'Smaller' Banks Buy and Sell Federal Funds." *Business Conditions,* Federal Reserve Bank of Chicago (August, 1965), pp. 8-12.

————. *Trading Federal Funds: Findings of a Three-Year Survey.* Washington: Board of Governors, September, 1965.

"Reserve Management at Fifth District Member Banks." *Monthly Review,* Federal Reserve Bank of Richmond (September, 1966), pp. 2-8.

"The Role of Twelfth District Banks in the Federal Funds Market: A Rising Factor in a Dynamic Market." *Monthly Review,* Federal Reserve Bank of San Francisco (June, 1961), pp. 104-21.

Roosa, Robert V. *Federal Reserve Operations in the Money and Government Securities Markets.* New York: Federal Reserve Bank of New York, 1956.

Rothwell, Jack C. "Federal Funds and the Profits Squeeze -- A New Awareness at Country Banks." *Business Review,* Federal Reserve Bank of Philadelphia (March, 1965), pp. 3-11.

Shull, Bernard. *Reappraisal of the Federal Reserve Discount Mechanism. Report on Research Undertaken in Connection with a System Study.* Washington: Board of Governors, August, 1968.

Toby, Jacob Allan. "Fed Funds: The Western Market." *Monthly Review,* Federal Reserve Bank of San Francisco (September, 1966), pp. 159-64.

"Trading in Bank Reserves." *Monthly Business Review,* Federal Reserve Bank of Cleveland (December, 1960), pp. 2-8.

"Trading in Federal Funds." *Monthly Business Review,* Federal Reserve Bank of Cleveland (October, 1961), pp. 8-10.

Willes, Mark H. "Federal Funds During Tight Money." *Business Review,* Federal Reserve Bank of Philadelphia (November, 1967), pp. 3-8.

Public Documents

U.S. Congress. Joint Economic Committee. *Employment, Growth, and Price Levels. Hearings,* Parts 6B and 6C: *The Government's Management of Its Monetary, Fiscal and Debt Operations.* 86th Cong., 1st sess., 1959.

U.S. Congress. Joint Economic Committee. *A Study of the Dealer Market for Federal Government Securities.* Materials prepared for the Joint Economic Committee. 86th Cong., 2d sess., 1960.

U.S. Congress. Senate. Committee on Banking and Currency. *Operation of the National and Federal Reserve Banking System. Hearings* before a subcommittee of the Senate Committee on Banking and Currency. 71st Cong., 3d sess., 1931, p. 96; and Appendix, Part 6, *Federal Reserve Questionnaires,* pp. 725-26.

U.S. Treasury. *Treasury-Federal Reserve Study of the Government Securities Market.* Washington, 1959 -- Part I, pp. 30-40 and Part III, pp. 67-91; and 1969 -- Part IV, pp. 14-15.

Unpublished Material

Brandt, Harry, and Crowe, Paul A. *Trading in Federal Funds by Banks in the Southeast.* Paper prepared for the Annual Meeting of the Southern Finance Association, New Orleans, November 18, 1967.

Calvert, E. Parker. *Federal Funds and Their Relation to Interbank Transfers and Payments.* Thesis, Graduate School of Banking, American Bankers Association, Rutgers University, June, 1952.

Healy, John. *Short-Term Investment Practices of Nonfinancial Corporations.* Masters Thesis, Massachusetts Institute of Technology, June, 1960.

Martens, Edward J. *Federal Funds -- A Money Market Device.* Thesis, Pacific Coast Banking School, Western Bankers Association, University of Washington, April, 1958.

Nichols, Dorothy M. *Federal Funds as a Tool of Bank Management.* Paper presented at the meeting of the Midwest Economic Association, Chicago, April 17, 1964.

Shertzer, Richard R. *San Francisco Banks and the Federal Funds Market.* Masters Thesis, University of California - Berkeley, February, 1957.

Pamphlets

Block, Ernest. *Eurodollars: An Emerging International Money Market.* The Bulletin, No. 39, New York: C. J. Devine Institute of Finance, New York University, April, 1966.

Garvin, Bantel & Co. *Money Market Memo.* New York: Garvin, Bantel & Co., March, 1964.

Johnson, Norris O. *Eurodollars in the New International Money Market.* New York: First National City Bank, July, 1964.

Morgan Guaranty Trust Company. *The Financing of Business with Euro-Dollars.* New York: Morgan Guaranty Trust Company, September, 1967.

_____. *Money Market Investment: The Risk and the Return.* New York: Morgan Guaranty Trust Company, April, 1964.

[Reierson, Roy L.] *The Euro-Dollar Market.* New York: Bankers Trust Company, July, 1964.